"This is all that we've come to expect and enjoy from Paul Tripp—a daily, fresh delivery of gospel comfort and hope. This will help us all to deepen our sense of appreciation and wonder at what Jesus has done for us."

Sam Allberry, Speaker, Ravi Zacharias International Ministries; Associate Pastor, Immanuel Church, Nashville, Tennessee; author, *7 Myths about Singleness*

"Paul Tripp has once again led us past feel-good platitudes and into focused, Christward reflection. Through tension and tenderness, lament and thanksgiving, the Lenten season will transform us when it leads us to the cross of Christ."

Ruth Chou Simons, Founder, GraceLaced Co.; author, *GraceLaced* and *Beholding and Becoming*; coauthor, *Foundations*

"Like so many others, I have benefited richly, and for years, from the ministry and writing of Paul Tripp. This latest work is no exception. *Journey to the Cross* is a precious reminder—one worth returning to again and again—of not only the rich benefits we receive through Christ's humiliation, death, and burial, but also of his dignifying invitation to properly lament the wrong that is in the world and the wrong that is within us. The season of Lent is a special, forty-day season to enable and empower God's people to do just that, and Tripp has provided us with a remarkable roadmap for the journey. I can't recommend this wonderful resource highly enough."

Scott Sauls, Senior Pastor, Christ Presbyterian Church, Nashville, Tennessee; author, *Jesus Outside the Lines* and *A Gentle Answer*

"I can't imagine volunteering to take a journey toward a place of gruesome execution. Who would? But that is the kind of passage that Lent asks of us every year: a journey of evaluation, examination, and blessed humiliation that leads to new life and increased joy. So, if we must traverse this path, then I don't know anyone whom I'd rather have as my tour guide than my brother, Paul Tripp. Through his decades of soul care, his transparent faith, and his deep love of God and his word, you'll find yourself learning to stop, to listen, and ultimately to worship the one who walked this path before you."

Elyse M. Fitzpatrick, coauthor, *Worthy: Celebrating the Value of Women*

"*Journey to the Cross* encourages us to be honest about our sin and embrace the cross of Christ, where we find mercy, grace, and salvation. As we linger on our need for a Savior, we're prompted to rejoice again in the hope that we have in Jesus. I look forward to reading this beautiful devotional by Paul Tripp in every Lenten season."

Hunter Beless, Founder and Executive Director, *Journeywomen* podcast

"This book understood me so well and convicted me so much I almost had to stop reading after day nine! Paul Tripp powerfully brings many truths home in this journey of reflections on God's love at the cross. Perhaps the most relevant is the desperately needed good news that there is a godly appropriateness in mourning for a broken world and for our own broken and sinful hearts. We can mourn in earnest because God has compassion. We can mourn with confident hope because Christ works in our mourning to grow us into the joy of victory over sin."

J. Alasdair Groves, Executive Director, Christian Counseling & Educational Foundation; coauthor, *Untangling Emotions*

"The greatest feasts are anticipated, and accentuated, by preceding fasts. Advent waits for Christmas, and when it comes, it is all the sweeter. And Lent—the long, winding, forty-day wilderness journey through the valley of the shadow of death—prepares our souls for the highest joys of the year, marking the greatest day in the history of the world so far: resurrection Sunday. For years both my wife and I have been guided, strengthened, and renewed by the ministry of Paul Tripp, as an instrument in God's redeeming hands. It's both encouraging and sobering now to have this help from Tripp for the bittersweet trek along the path of Lent."

David Mathis, Senior Teacher and Executive Editor, desiringGod.org; Pastor, Cities Church, Saint Paul, Minnesota; author, *Habits of Grace: Enjoying Jesus through the Spiritual Disciplines*

"It's incredible. Time and time again, Paul Tripp's insightful reflections on Scripture help bring God's truth into the here and now of daily life. Tripp brilliantly and gracefully illuminates why the Lenten season is so important as it points us to the greatest act of love in all of history. *Journey to the Cross* is Paul Tripp's writing at its absolute best—I loved this book and you will too."

Shelby Abbott, author, *DoubtLess* and *Pressure Points*; speaker; campus minister

JOURNEY
TO THE
CROSS

Paul David Tripp Books

JOURNEY TO THE CROSS

A 40-DAY LENTEN DEVOTIONAL

PAUL DAVID TRIPP

:: CROSSWAY®

WHEATON, ILLINOIS

Lyrics from "Nothing but the Blood of Jesus," by Robert Lowry, 1876, are cited in Day 38.

Cover design and illustration: Jordan Singer

First printing 2021

Printed in China

Scripture quotations are from the ESV® Bible (The Holy Bible, English Standard Version®), copyright © 2001 by Crossway, a publishing ministry of Good News Publishers. Used by permission. All rights reserved.

Hardcover ISBN: 978-1-4335-6767-4
ePub ISBN: 978-1-4335-6770-4
PDF ISBN: 978-1-4335-6768-1
Mobipocket ISBN: 978-1-4335-6769-8

Library of Congress Cataloging-in-Publication Data

Names: Tripp, Paul David, 1950– author.
Title: Journey to the cross : a 40-day Lenten devotional / Paul David Tripp.
Description: Wheaton, Illinois : Crossway, 2021. | Includes bibliographical references and index.
Identifiers: LCCN 2020007248 (print) | LCCN 2020007249 (ebook) | ISBN 9781433567674 (hardcover) | ISBN 9781433567681 (pdf) | ISBN 9781433567698 (mobipcket) | ISBN 9781433567704 (epub)
Subjects: LCSH: Lent—Prayers and devotions.
Classification: LCC BV85 .T665 2021 (print) | LCC BV85 (ebook) | DDC 242./34—dc23
LC record available at https://lccn.loc.gov/2020007248
LC ebook record available at https://lccn.loc.gov/2020007249

Crossway is a publishing ministry of Good News Publishers.

RRDS		31	30	29	28	27	26	25	24	23	22	21
15	14	13	12	11	10	9	8	7	6	5	4	3	2	1

INTRODUCTION

It's good to mourn, it's healthy to be sad, and it's appropriate to groan. Something is wrong with us, something is missing in our hearts and our understanding of life, if we are able to look around and look inside and not grieve. You don't have to look very far to see that we live, work, and relate in a world that has been twisted and bent by sin, so much so that it doesn't function at all in the way God intended. The sin-scarred condition of the world is obvious in your home, your neighborhood, and your church. We see it in government, politics, business, education, entertainment, and the internet.

In Romans 8, Paul captures the sad condition of the world in three provocative phrases that should break our hearts:

"subjected to futility" (v. 20)
"its bondage to corruption" (v. 21)
"in the pains of childbirth" (v. 22)

We should be rejoicing people, because we have, in the redemption that is ours in Christ Jesus, eternal reason to rejoice. But this side of our final home, our rejoicing should be mixed with weeping as we witness, experience, and, sadly, give way to the presence and power of evil. Christ taught in his most lengthy recorded sermon, the Sermon on the Mount, that those who mourn are blessed, so it's important to understand why. Mourning means you recognize the most important reality in the human existence, sin. Mourning means you have been hit by the weight of what it has done to you and to everyone you know. Mourning says you have considered the devastating fact that life right here, right now, is one big spiritual war. Mourning means that you have come to realize, as you get up in the morning, that once again you will be greeted with a catalog of temptations. Mourning means you know that there really are spiritual enemies out there meaning to do you harm. Mourning results when you confess that there are places where your heart still wanders.

But mourning does something wonderful to you. The sad realities that cause you to mourn also cause you to cry out for the help, rescue, forgiveness, and deliverance of a Redeemer. Jesus said that if you mourn, you will be comforted. He's not talking about the comfort of elevated feelings. He's talking about the comfort of the presence and grace of a Redeemer, who meets you in your mourning, hears your cries for help, comes to you in saving mercy, and wraps arms of eternal love around you. It's the comfort of knowing that you're forgiven, being restored, now living in a reconciled relationship with the one who made you, and now living with your destiny secure.

Mourning sin—past, present, and future—is the first step in seeking and celebrating the divine grace that is the hope of everyone whose heart has been made able to see by that very same grace.

So it is right and beneficial to take a season of the year to reevaluate, recalibrate, and have the values of our hearts clarified once again. Lent is such a season. As we approach Holy Week, where we remember the sacrifice, suffering, and resurrection of our Savior, it's good to give ourselves to humble and thankful mourning. Lent is about remembering the suffering and sacrifice of the Savior. Lent is about confessing our ongoing battle with sin. Lent is about fasting, and not just from food; we willingly and joyfully let go of things in this world that have too much of a hold on us. And Lent is about giving ourselves in a more focused way to prayer, crying out for the help that we desperately need from the only one who is able to give it.

For forty days you can use this devotional as your stimulus and guide as you stop, consider, mourn, confess, pray, and give your heart to thanksgiving. May you step away from the tyranny of a busy life, with its seemingly endless demands, and consider the most important thing that's happened to you, your most important struggle, and the most wonderful gift that you have ever been given. And as you do this, may you open your heart and your hands and let go of things that you not only hold, but that have taken ahold of you. May this free you to seek your Savior more fully, to celebrate him more deeply, and to follow him more faithfully.

Together we will follow Jesus on his journey to the cross. The horrible, public sacrifice of Jesus should ignite not only our celebration, but also our mourning. The cross confronts us with who we really are (sinners) and what we need (rescuing and forgiving grace). How can you consider what Christ willingly suffered because of our sin and not mourn the sin that remains? How could you consider how lost you were and how spiritually needy you still are and not celebrate the grace of the cross? This will be a devotional of celebration and self-examination.

During our forty days together, may your mourning increase so that your joy may deepen. May you groan more so that you would pray more. May your sadness ignite your celebration. And may all of this result in blessings that are too big and too obvious to miss.

DAY 1

God is holy, so sin is serious. God is gracious, so sin can
be forgiven. On the cross his holiness and grace kiss.

O f all the events in my life, one is by far the most important. Of all the blessings in my life, one is without a doubt the most wonderful blessing of all. Of all the things I most needed, but could never provide for myself, this was my deepest need.

One summer my mom and dad decided to empty their house of their four children. I ended up with my younger brother at a children's camp in the middle of nowhere in northern Pennsylvania. It was a long way away for a long time for a nine-year-old boy. I remember dragging a heavy wooden locker that my dad had made up the long hill to my cabin. I was bunked in with a rowdy pack of eight- and nine-year-olds, whose faces would change at the beginning of each week.

I can remember being a bit upset that I had been assigned to the oldest male camp counselor on the staff. He didn't look athletic and he was a bit bald, so he looked ancient to me. I just knew he would be boring and strict and that I would be stuck with him that long hot summer. What I didn't know was that God was going to use that man to give me two wonderful gifts, gifts that we all need, whether we know it or not. That summer turned out to be the most significant, life-altering, and eternally important of my life.

I was being raised in an imperfect Christian home, and I carried with me a God-awareness from day one. My family attended church whenever the doors were opened and had family worship every morning. I knew every biblical story and could quote many key passages from memory, including the entire Christmas story as told in Luke 2. But the one thing I lacked was the knowledge of my own sin. I was the quintessential Christian-culture kid who was not a Christian. My problem was that I had no knowledge of the difference, and because I didn't, I had no sense of personal spiritual need. But at camp that would change dramatically and forever.

My old bald counselor decided that before our bedtime devotions each week he would teach his fidgety pack of nine-year-olds the first several chapters of Romans. So, I got Romans 1–5 over and over again that summer. God knew what I needed and put me right where I would get it. One particular night the words of Romans 3:23, "for all have sinned and fall short of the glory of God," cut like a knife into my heart. But I fought the conviction that gripped me and tried my best to hide the emotion that accompanied it.

I climbed into my third-tier bunk, but couldn't sleep, so I began to do what no nine-year-old boy ever wants to do in bed at camp: I began to cry. And I could not stop crying. I had been given an unexpected and undeserved gift, *the knowledge of my sin.* At nine years old, it gripped me, scared me, and would not let me go. I lay there crying and knew I needed to pray. Why? Because I had been given another gift: *the knowledge of a ready, willing, and capable Savior.* I had been blessed with the awareness of his offer of forgiveness to all who confess their sin and by faith seek his forgiveness.

In my tears, I had no idea how blessed I was. I had no idea of the horrible deceitfulness of sin. I had no idea of the natural self-righteousness that is in the heart of every sinner. I had no idea that most people have no idea how dark their condition actually is. I had no idea how skilled we sinners are at giving self-atoning arguments for what we have said and done, in an attempt to remove any real guilt for sin. I had no idea that I had been chosen and was being called to no longer be a cultural Christian, but a true child of God. I had no idea that the only thing in life more important than the knowledge of sin is the knowledge of the Savior's grace. And I had been given both. I had no idea that I had to experience the terrifying knowledge of sin, or I would never seek the Savior's forgiving grace.

What I did know was that I needed to pray. I needed to confess my sin and cry out for God's forgiveness. And I knew I needed to do it right there and then. But in my nine-year-old mind I thought it was disrespectful to pray such a significant prayer lying down. So I crawled out of my bunk and down the ladder as quietly as I could. I knelt in the middle of the stone floor and confessed my sin and placed my little-boy trust in the forgiving grace of the Savior. Then I quietly climbed back up to my bunk and fell fast asleep.

The Lenten season is about the sin that was the reason for the suffering and sacrifice of the Savior. It is about taking time to reflect on why we all needed such a radical move of redemption, to confess the hold that sin still has on us, and to focus on opening our hands, in confession and submission, and letting go of sin once again. But as we do this, it is important to remember that the knowledge of sin is not a dark and nasty thing but a huge and wonderful blessing. If you are aware of your sin, you are aware of it only because you have been visited by amazing grace. Don't resist that awareness. Silence your inner lawyer and all the self-defending arguments for your righteousness. Quit relieving your guilt by pointing a finger of blame at someone else. And stop telling yourself in the middle of a sermon that you know someone who really needs to hear it.

Be thankful that you have been chosen to bear the burden of the knowledge of sin, because that burden is what drove you and will continue to drive you to seek the help and rescue that only the Savior Jesus can give you. To see sin clearly is a sure sign of God's grace. Be thankful.

Reflection Questions ————————————————————

1. In a typical week, how aware are you of the depth of your sin? When was the last time you wept over your sin?

2. Do you usually view the conviction of the Spirit as a blessing to be pursued or a burden to be avoided? Why?

3. What habits and disciplines help you foster an inner spirit of confession and repentance?

Read and meditate on Psalm 51:1–12, using it as a template for a time of confession.

DAY 2

*When the shadow of the cross hangs over us, we
are not surprised by sin, and we are not afraid
to look at what has already been forgiven.*

My sin seemed to sneak up on me again, like a stalker jumping out from behind the bushes. I was unprepared, but why? I was surprised, but shouldn't have been. The instant change in my thinking, desires, and emotions was shocking. I got angry in a situation where my anger was unexpected. Instead of wanting to serve, I suddenly wanted to win, to be affirmed as right. My voice got louder, my tone got sharper, and my face reddened. My ability to communicate turned from a tool of help to a weapon of offense. I said unkind things and other things in an unkind way. At that moment, I was a self-appointed king, the universe shrunk to the size of my desires, and all I wanted was for my will to be done. And as I was sinning, I was already erecting self-atoning arguments that would make my sin acceptable to my conscience. But it wasn't long before remorse came, and by God's grace confession followed.

Open your heart to what I am about to say next. My story is your story too. Whether you're standing in your teenager's bedroom, sitting with your computer on your lap, plodding through work, or rushing through the grocery store, sin creeps up on you and seizes you. Before you know it, you're in its hold. Later you look back with regret. You tell yourself that you'll do better next time, only to get kidnapped again a little further down the road. This is the sadly repeating drama of all of us living between the "already" and the "not yet."

This is why it is important to dedicate a season of every year to sit under the shadow of the cross of Jesus Christ once again. Under the shadow of the cross, sin doesn't surprise us anymore, doesn't depress us anymore, and doesn't move us to deny or defend. Under the shadow of the cross, we remember who we are and what it is that we are dealing with. Under the shadow of the cross, we are required to admit that the greatest enemy we face is not difficulty or maltreatment from without, but the enemy of sin within. Under the shadow of the cross, we quit pointing fingers and begin crying out for help. Under the shadow of the cross, we are reminded that we are not in this battle alone; in fact, there we admit that we have no power whatsoever to battle on our own. Under the shadow of the cross we get our sanity back, admitting who we are and what it is that we so desperately need. The shadow of the cross is a place of peace and protection that can be found nowhere else. Let the shadow of the cross be your teacher.

1. The shadow of the cross teaches us who we are. We all need to stop again and again and let the cross remind us of who we are, and in reminding us, to humble us anew. We do tend to think of ourselves more highly than we ought. Here's what happens to many of us. When we first come to Christ, we are very aware of our sin, and therefore we carry with us a constant desire for God's help. But as saving grace gets our lives into order and we are following, fellowshiping, and obeying, we begin to let go of that sense of need. We begin to think of ourselves as okay—and in one sense we are, because our salvation is sealed once and for all. On the other hand, as long as sin still lurks inside us, we are not okay and are still in constant need of redeeming grace. Sitting under the shadow of the cross shatters the delusion that we are free of the need of what originally brought us to Jesus: divine grace.

2. The shadow of the cross teaches what we need. The cross powerfully reminds me that I need much more than situational, relational, financial, or physical change. The cross is the ultimate diagnostic. It accurately puts its finger on the ultimate disease, and then offers the only reliable cure. Accurate diagnosis is always necessary for there to be a real, lasting cure. Bad diagnosis will prevent cure from happening. Your inner lawyer, your friends, and your culture may tell you that your biggest problem is not you, and they may tell you that all you need to do is move, quit, find new friends, get a new job, or make more money; but each one of those is a misdiagnosis. These things will not treat the disease that has you in its grip. Only grace can do that. The cross preaches that sin is our problem and that rescuing, forgiving, transforming, and delivering grace is the only medicine that will provide the cure we all need.

3. The shadow of the cross teaches us who God is. The cross tells us that God is unrelentingly merciful. It is amazing to think that he would control all the things that he needed to control so that Jesus would arrive on that awful cross as an acceptable sacrifice for our redemption! The cross preaches God's saving zeal, his boundless love, and his willingness to unleash his almighty power and unlimited sovereignty to draw rebels to himself. The cross teaches us that God doesn't look at sinners with disdain or disgust, but with generous and tender love. The cross teaches us that we do not have to clean ourselves up to come to God; we only need to come in humble confession. The cross teaches us that when we sin, God doesn't greet us with a sentence of condemnation, but with a reminder once again of the completeness of his pardon. The cross allows unholy people to look in the face of a holy God and have hope.

4. *The shadow of the cross teaches us what God offers us.* The cross teaches us that God offers us the one thing that no other person or thing can. He offers us the grace of forgiveness. He offers us the grace of welcome into relationship with him. He offers us the grace of personal transformation. He offers us the grace of a new identity and new potential. He offers us the grace of a glorious and fully secured destiny. Yes, it is true, he offers us grace upon grace!

5. *The shadow of the cross teaches us how we should live.* The cross teaches us that we should live humbly wise. It's foolish and prideful to be unprepared for the battle with sin. Unpreparedness denies all that the cross teaches us about who we are and what we need. The cross teaches us that we need to pray for eyes to see and hearts that are attentive to the enemy's temptations and sin's lies. The cross teaches us to be humbly ready and to start every day with cries for divine rescue and strength.

6. The shadow of the cross gives us hope and courage. The cross teaches us to be unafraid to admit and confess sin, not because we are powerful or capable, but because Jesus is the victor, and there is nothing that we will ever face inside or outside us that exists outside the circle of the completed victory of the cross. I can face my sin without depression or panic because he battled for me and won and continues to do so.

It really is a good thing to sit under the shadow of the cross for a season, to consider, confess, and rest once again.

Reflection Questions ———————————————————————

1. What do you think it means to live under the shadow of the cross? What are some practical ways to get yourself there?

2. Do you agree that your greatest problem is your sin? What attitudes or actions in your life suggest that maybe you don't truly believe that?

3. Think of some of the things you need right now, either materially or spiritually. How might placing yourself in the shadow of the cross inform or enhance your perspective on those needs?

Read Psalm 130, and note what the psalmist says about who we are and who God is. Use this psalm to guide your prayer time today.

DAY 3

*Keep reminding yourself that you live in a world
that is groaning, waiting for redemption, but
remind yourself also that the cross guarantees
that the groaning will someday end.*

Permit yourself to groan; you have valid reasons to do so. Give
yourself to seasons of groaning; it is spiritually healthy to do
so. And as you groan, remember that your Lord hears your groaning and responds with tender loving care. Now, it is important to
note that most of our groaning is not only spiritually unhealthy;
it is spiritually debilitating. We most often groan because we have
not gotten our own way or because something or someone has
gotten in our way. Often our groaning is little more than verbal
pouting. It is a symptom of our continuing desire to be sovereign so as to guarantee that we will get the pleasures, treasures,
and comforts that we have set our hearts on. Sadly, so much of
our groaning is self-oriented frustration that ends up making us
despondent, discouraged, and a bit bitter.

But we have reason to groan because we live in a world that is breaking under the harsh burden of the destructiveness of sin. Every day we are greeted by corporate sin, cultural sin, institutional sin, and individual sin. Sin never has a good harvest. Sin always deceives, divides, and destroys. It always promises what it can't deliver and delivers things that were not part of the bargain. Sin masquerades as something it is not and can never be. It is the ultimate wolf in sheep's clothing. It has left both humanity and the surrounding creation broken and crippled.

Think about when we typically groan. We groan when we're disappointed. We groan when we're grieving. We groan when we're in pain. We groan when we're frustrated. We groan when we feel weak. We groan when we're exhausted. We groan when things are not the way they are supposed to be. It's right to groan for the right reason. It's right to be sad at what sin has done to you and everything around you. It's good to be frustrated when you've allowed yourself once again to be hoodwinked by sin. It's good to groan at how sin makes marriage difficult and parenting a travail. It's good to mourn the effect of sin on the church and the workplace, on education and government. It's good to groan when the spiritual battle has left you tired and wounded. It's right to groan when you see loved ones trapped in sin's deceit.

Here's what is important to understand: your groaning is either anger that you've not gotten your way or a cry that God would get his holy, loving, wise, and righteous way. Groaning is either, "Will my kingdom ever come?" or it is, "Your kingdom come." It is good to stop and examine your groaning and to give yourself to a season of the right kind of groaning. After all, you do live in a groaning place. Paul says it this way in Romans 8:22: "For we know that the whole creation has been groaning together in pains of childbirth until now."

But it's tempting to avoid groaning, to keep yourself too busy or too distracted to be able to think about your struggle with sin and the brokenness of the world around you. It's tempting to try to convince yourself that you are okay and the things around you are not that bad. It's tempting to numb your heart with the physical pleasures of this fallen world. It's tempting to put on a happy face when you're not really happy or happy with how you're doing. It's tempting to give nonanswers or evasive answers when someone asks you how you're doing. It's tempting to try to convince yourself to feel good about things that are not good. It's tempting to work at not groaning.

So, it takes grace to groan over sin internal and external. It's counterintuitive to do so. At the point of sinning, sin doesn't look horrible; it looks attractive. When you're lusting, you don't see danger; you see beauty. When you're gossiping, you don't think about its destructiveness, because you're carried away by the buzz of carrying a tale. When you are overeating, you don't see the sin in what you're doing, because you are enjoying the pleasure of the sights and tastes of the food. When you're cheating on your taxes, you don't think about the danger of a heart that has become comfortable with thievery, because you're caught up into thinking about how you will spend the money gained. Part of the deceitfulness of sin is its ability to make what is destructive appear attractive.

When you are groaning sin's destruction, you are groaning because you've been blessed with eyes that see clearly, a mind that thinks wisely, and a heart that has been made tender by grace. The problem is not that we groan, but that we groan selfishly or we do not groan at all. Grace will make you groan and then will turn your groaning into rejoicing. In your groaning, you rejoice because you know that God meets you in your groaning. The apostle Paul says that God hears and answers even when we are without words with which to groan (see Rom. 8:26–27). You see, we are not just groaning into the air as some cathartic exercise. No, we groan to someone who has invited us to groan and has promised to hear and to answer. We groan to one who is in us, with us, and for us, who has blessed us with life-altering promises and who will not quit working on our behalf until we have no more reason to groan. We groan to one who has already won the victory over everything for which we groan and who will not rest until all his children are experiencing all the fruits of that victory. In this way our groaning is not selfish anger, but a cry for help to the only one who has the power, authority, wisdom, and grace to come to our aid and give us what we really need. And in our groaning, we confess that too often we groan for the wrong reason.

So, stop and groan. Let your heart feel the burden of the full weight of sin both internal and external. Scan your life, scan your heart, scan your thoughts and desires, scan your words and behavior, scan the struggles of the people around you, scan the world you live in, and find reason to groan. Let sin's sadness drive you once again to the cross where your Savior groaned aloud on your behalf as he bore the horrible weight of sin. Take time to let sadness sink in so it may lead you to redemption's celebration, as you remember that the debt has been paid and the ultimate victory over what makes you groan has been guaranteed.

Yes, indeed, it is good to groan.

Reflection Questions ——————————————————

1. Thinking of both the subject of your groaning and its effects, how can you tell whether your groaning is spiritually healthy or spiritually unhealthy?

2. In what ways do you find it challenging to engage with spiritual lament?

3. How could you more effectively groan over your sin, and what spiritual benefits might that offer?

Read Psalm 74, and then use it as a catalyst for writing your own song of lament. Include both private and corporate confession and need.

DAY 4

God intends suffering to pry open our hands so we let go
of the things of this earth and hold more tightly to Jesus.

What has you in its hold? Don't rush to answer. Stop and give this question some consideration.

What do you feel you can't live without?

What has the ability to make or break your day?

What has the power to make you very sad?

What can produce almost instant happiness?

The loss of what would leave you a bit depressed?

What do you tend to attach your identity to?

What tends to control your wishes?

What do others have that causes you to envy?

If you could get just one thing, what would it be?

The absence of what tempts you to question God's goodness?

What does your use of money tell you about what's important to you?

What fills your fantasies and your dreams?

What would the videos of your last six weeks reveal about what has you in its hold?

What physical idols tempt you most?

What relational idols attract you the most?

Is there a place where you're asking the creation to do what only the Creator can?

Lent is an important tool in the inescapable battle that rages in all our hearts between worship and service of the Creator and worship and service of the creation. Lent calls us to remember once again that sin reduces us all to idolaters somehow, someway. It gives us a season to take time and reflect on things that have taken too strong a hold on us, things that we have come to crave too strongly and love too dearly. It reminds us that often things that we are holding tightly have actually taken an even tighter hold on us.

Here's the core of the struggle: as long as sin still resides in our hearts, we will have an inclination to ask the physical creation to do for us what the Creator alone is able to do. Everyone is in search of true and lasting joy. Everyone wants peace of heart. Everyone wants to be content. Everyone is searching for life. Everyone wants to be deeply, fully, and perfectly loved. Everyone wants a heart that is satisfied. So everyone is on a quest to find these things even when they don't know they are. Everyone looks for identity. Everyone searches for something that will give them meaning and purpose. Everyone searches for something to hook their hope to. In this way everyone is born searching for God. They just don't know it.

Because creation is so obvious (you can see it, you can taste it, you can feel it, and you can smell it), it's tempting to look to it to deliver all the things for which we are all searching. But satisfaction of our hearts is not the purpose of the physical creation; it actually has a much higher purpose. Creation was made to point us to the one who alone has the power to satisfy our longing hearts. He is the bread that will satisfy our hunger. He is the living water that makes us thirst no longer. With every vista, on every day, with every new experience and each new look, creation has been designed to point us to God.

But there's even more to think about here. Looking to creation to do what it was not meant to do will not only disappoint us; it will enslave us. Idols never just disappoint us; they addict us as well. Because the buzz of joy that creation gives us is so short, we have to go back again and again, and soon we're convinced we cannot live without the next hit. What we tightly hold onto takes hold of us, now commanding of us what only God should ever command: our hearts. And what holds our hearts will dictate our words and behavior.

It is possible to think that you are a God-worshiper because he is the object of your formal religious worship, but when it comes to the day-by-day affections of your heart, something or someone else could be in control. And it's not always that we are under the control of evil things. Often good things have control over us that they should not have. As I have written elsewhere, good things become bad things when they become ruling things.*

---

* Paul David Tripp, *Parenting: 14 Gospel Principals That Can Radically Change Your Family* (Wheaton, IL: Crossway, 20), 81.

So how about letting yourself suffer loss for a season? Let go of things you tend to prize. Let this season of sacrifice loosen your hands and free your heart. Let go of some of your comforts, things that have perhaps comforted you too much, so that your heart is free to seek a better Comforter. Pray that a season of going without will refocus your eyes and reposition your heart. God is good at using seasons of suffering to cause us to let go of our dependency on created things and reach out in dependency to our Creator, Savior, and Lord.

May this season's discomforts lead us to find lasting comfort in him.

Reflection Questions ───────────────────────────

1. Spend some time meditating on and perhaps journaling about the diagnostic questions from the devotional. Based on that exercise, what are some idols you are tempted to bow down to?

2. What things do you ask the physical creation to do that only God can do? If you're stumped, take a look at where you seek pleasure and what causes conflict in your closest relationships.

3. Now you are ready to answer the real question: What do you need to give up, for a season or more permanently, to root the idols out of your heart?

Read Luke 9:23–25 and Romans 6:1–14, and prayerfully consider what you might give up during this season of Lent as a way to find your comfort in Christ.

DAY 5

Prayer is abandoning my righteousness,
admitting my need for forgiveness, and resting
in the grace of the cross of Jesus Christ.

Prayer is one of God's sweetest gifts to us. The command to pray is itself a sweet and loving gift from a gracious and caring heavenly Father. Prayer is where God welcomes his children to talk with him, commune with him, abide with him. It's that holy place where the deepest of worship, the deepest of needs, and the most honest of confessions all intersect with the grandeur and glory of divine love. Prayer only works when worshipers are invited into the presence of one worthy of their worship. It only works when the one being prayed to is amazingly patient, boundless in love, constantly forgiving, and sovereign in power. For prayer to be prayer, God has to be God; without this, prayer is an act of religious futility.

But God is God, and he has invited us to bring our true selves to him. It's not an invitation to bring him a catalog of our self-oriented desires, as if he were little more than a cosmic delivery system for whatever cravings consume us at the moment. No, the heart of prayer is worshipful submission to him, which produces gratitude, humility, vision, and willingness in us. Without adoration and submission, prayer is reduced to a set of demands that make it look as if we are gods, and God's job is to submit his almighty power to our lordship. It is shocking to consider that what appears to be our most conscious Godward act can actually be evidence of our ongoing idolatry.

So prayer is spiritual warfare. To pray we need rescuing grace that will free us from the dominion of our own selfish hearts. To get our hearts to that counterintuitive place of adoration and submission we need the help of the one to whom we pray. It's hard to pray true "Your kingdom come, your will be done" prayers and even harder to pray these kinds of prayers on the fly. It's counterintuitive to confess that what I need most is not all the things my heart tends to desire. It's hard to confess that what I need most is redeeming grace. So prayer is a fight. Prayer takes work. Prayer calls us to go to places we don't often go and give our hearts to do what we do too infrequently.

Of course you should take ample time to pray every day. Prayer is a powerful weapon in the spiritual war for your heart that wages every day of your life on this side of forever. But it is also good to give yourself to seasons of prayer. Lent could be one of those seasons where you take time to meditate, examine, and consider. Here are four categories that can organize this season of worship for you.

Adoration. Give yourself to meditate on all the reasons the Lord is worthy of your worship. Make time to take in the full grandeur of his majesty, the amazing extent of his love, the unending zeal of his grace, his incalculable power, the completeness of his sovereignty, the extent of his patience, his ever-operating mercy, the depth of his wisdom, and the pristine perfection of his holiness. As a preparation for adoring prayer, study his word again and let your heart be taken up once again with his splendor. Here you let him loom large in your eyes and place the shadow of his glory over your heart. Here you pray his glory back to him in words of praise that you know fall short of capturing his glory even as you pray them. Adoration stimulates the kind of worship that is not just a sacrifice of words, but the offer of your life to this glorious Lord.

Confession. Confession follows adoration, because the more you gaze upon God, the more you will see yourself with accuracy and the more you will mourn what you see. When Isaiah in his vision stood before the holiness of the Lord, his first words weren't, "Wow, this is amazing!" No, his first words were, "Woe is me! For I am lost; for I am a man of unclean lips, and I dwell in the midst of a people of unclean lips; for my eyes have seen the King, the LORD of hosts!" (Isa. 6:5). It takes a vision of God to have a true and reliable vision of ourselves. We are so often blinded by our own righteousness that it takes the unblemished righteousness of God to expose to us the true degree of our own unrighteousness. Prayer doesn't just include studying our Lord so that we would be overwhelmed by his glory; we also examine ourselves and the many reasons we have to confess our weaknesses, failures, and sin. And confession only works when the one receiving the confession is forgiving and has the power and willingness to rescue and restore. So come in confession, because the cross assures us of our Lord's willingness to forgive.

Submission. "Not my will, but yours, be done" is the heart of true prayer. Prayer is submitting the desires of your heart to a kingdom greater than your own. Prayer is submitting your requests to a plan that is greater than the one you have for yourself. Prayer is giving yourself to a set of rules you didn't make up. Prayer is surrendering your gifts to the glory of someone else. Prayer is so much more than asking; at the center is submitting. So we ask for the grace to submit because, as we have already confessed, we do not have the desire, willingness, or power to do so on our own.

Supplication. Finally, prayer is where limited, weak, and failing worshipers bring their needs before the one who is with them, in them, and for them, and who is delighted to meet those needs. Having already submitted ourselves to the mission of his kingship, we now bring before our Lord prayers that are consistent with that heart of submission. And because we have submitted ourselves to plans and purposes that are bigger than us, we don't pray just for ourselves but also for others. Our supplications are not individual and narrow, but are as wide and as huge as his kingdom is.

How about giving yourself to forty days of this kind of prayer, with all the study and meditation it requires? And know that as you do, God is tender, gracious, and understanding. He receives our messy prayers. He hears those brief prayers on the fly. He doesn't reject prayers that reflect inaccurate theology or those prayed in moments when we really don't know how to pray. Weak, faltering prayers are received by him and warmly answered. But he invites us into something deeper and better. He invites us into something that we could never earn or deserve on our own. He invites us into willing, adoring, restful communion with him. Why wouldn't you accept that invitation?

Reflection Questions ———————————————————

1. Does your typical pattern of prayer reflect the reality that "the heart of prayer is worshipful submission" to God? How might your prayers change if you really embraced this definition of prayer?

2. How well do your prayers balance the four categories of prayer: adoration, confession, submission, and supplication? Which area do you tend to shortchange, and what are some practical things you can do to grow in that area?

3. True spiritual warfare-type prayers require study and meditation. What can you do in this Lenten season to give yourself more fully to these tasks?

Pray slowly through the Lord's Prayer in Matthew 6:9–13, focusing on adoration, confession, submission, and supplication.

DAY 6

The empty tomb stands as an eternal promise
to you that God will always finish what
he has begun in you and for you.

It is important to remember that at the end of Lent stands a tomb. From the moment he was born, Jesus was marching to his death. He had to be willing to suffer and die in order for redemption to be accomplished and applied. Death was his job description. Death was his destiny. But death was not his defeat, because death was not the end of the story of the Messiah Jesus. What looked like the ultimate victory of evil over good, what looked like a crushing defeat and a sad end to the redemptive story, was, in reality, the greatest victory of divine power and grace that the world had ever seen. The Messiah had come. In his perfectly righteous life, he had conquered sin, but that was not enough. The hope of humanity hung on the question of whether or not he had the power to defeat the ultimate enemy, death. The empty tomb was a glorious answer to that question. The empty tomb is a promise that God will never leave his redemptive work half done. He will complete everything that needs to be done for his chosen children to experience the full range of the blessings of his grace.

What I am going to say next may surprise you; it may even discourage you. But I will explain the importance of this surprising statement. At the end of Lent is *your* death, as well. During this season, more than any other, we focus on and contemplate the shocking, cruel death of the only perfect person who ever lived. We meditate on his willingness to die, on the essentiality of that death, and on its benefit to all who put their trust in the Lord Jesus Christ. Death is the motif of this season of remembrance. It is the motif not just because of the death of Jesus, but because, during this season, we hear again another call to die. Death is required of every follower of the Lord Jesus Christ. Knowing the full range of the benefits of the new life that the resurrection of Jesus promises us *requires that we too die*. In the gospel we come to understand that death is the inescapable pathway to life. Consider these passages:

> And [Jesus] said to all, "If anyone would come after me, let him deny himself and take up his cross daily and follow me." (Luke 9:23)

> For whoever would save his life will lose it, but whoever loses his life for my sake and the gospel's will save it. (Mark 8:35)

> Truly, truly, I say to you, unless a grain of wheat falls into the earth and dies, it remains alone; but if it dies, it bears much fruit. (John 12:24)

And whoever does not take his cross and follow me is not worthy of me. (Matt. 10:38)

I have been crucified with Christ. It is no longer I who live, but Christ who lives in me. And the life I now live in the flesh I live by faith in the Son of God, who loved me and gave himself for me. (Gal. 2:20)

What shall we say then? Are we to continue in sin that grace may abound? By no means! How can we who died to sin still live in it? Do you not know that all of us who have been baptized into Christ Jesus were baptized into his death? We were buried therefore with him by baptism into death, in order that, just as Christ was raised from the dead by the glory of the Father, we too might walk in newness of life. (Rom. 6:1–4)

He himself bore our sins in his body on the tree, that we might die to sin and live to righteousness. By his wounds you have been healed. (1 Pet. 2:24)

I protest, brothers, by my pride in you, which I have in Christ Jesus our Lord, I die every day! (1 Cor. 15:31)

I appeal to you therefore, brothers, by the mercies of God, to present your bodies as a living sacrifice, holy and acceptable to God, which is your spiritual worship. (Rom. 12:1)

The gospel offers you something that nothing and no one else can offer: life. But in offering life, the gospel calls you to die. That death is both an event and a process. By God's redeeming plan we are united with Christ in his death and resurrection. In that way your moment of belief is a death and a resurrection. But there is more. Now that you are united with Christ, you are called to a very specific surrender, that is, dying to self. You simply cannot understand the gospel without this call to follow Christ in his death. We are called to die to sin.

We are called to die to that life where we did what we wanted to do, when we wanted to do it, and how we wanted to do it. We are called to die to setting our own rules and living however we please. We are called to die to our rulership of our own lives. We are called to let go of our self-appointed sovereignty, living as if we're the only master that we need, and to surrender ourselves and all we have to another master. We are called to die to our desires for our own comfort, pleasure, and glory and give ourselves to seek the glory of the King and the success of his kingdom. We are called to die to our own righteousness and find our hope, help, and comfort in the righteousness of Jesus given over to our account. This death that I have just described is a process of daily scanning our lives to see where things still live in us that should not live, then praying for the strength to die once again.

Like the death of Jesus, this death is not a defeat, but a huge and glorious victory. For everywhere you die, you will be resurrected to new life in that area. It is the continuing resurrection/transformation/liberation work of sanctifying grace. So this season, how about scanning your heart and life? How about looking for those places where you still need to die to self? How about crying out for the willingness to take up your cross and follow

Jesus in his death? How about celebrating the fact that dying to self is never a defeat, but another step in the ongoing victories of grace that can be yours because you have been united with Jesus in his death and resurrection?

Lent calls you to die, and that is a very good thing!

Reflection Questions

1. How do you react to the assertion that "at the end of Lent is your death"? Does that sentence make you feel burdened or relieved—and why?

2. Where have you seen victory come out of death in your own life?

3. What areas of your life need to die to make room for greater, more abundant life in Christ?

Read Romans 12:1–2, and consider what sacrifices God is calling you to make as an act of worship.

DAY 7

*In this broken world we won't get paradise now,
but the empty tomb guarantees us that a new
heaven and new earth are in our future.*

Paradise is the constant hope of all of us. It is hardwired within us. We tend to look for it everywhere. Our vain search heaps piles of disappointment on us. Our dream is shattered again and again, sometimes by the same thing over again. We find it hard to be satisfied, and we are tempted to become bitter. We know we should have learned our lesson, but then we get up and start searching again. Somehow, in some way, every human being is searching for paradise. We look for it in the children we parent. We look for it in the houses we buy. We look for it in our friendships. We look for it in our jobs. We hope we'll get it in our marriages. We hope a vacation will give us just a little bit of it. We envy people who we think have found it (although no one has). We think if we just have a little more power, we will find it. We hope another academic degree will be a pathway to it. We move to a new city hoping more of it will be there than in the last. We hop from church to church, hoping we'll find it there. We're emotionally exhausted, but we keep searching.

Paradise is the world as it was meant to be, everything in order, nothing threatening anything or anyone else, perfect harmony between God and humanity. No sickness or suffering, creation and Creator in perfect cooperation, all needs met, all desires balanced, hearts and minds not only pure, but content. We were created for such a world, but like a beautifully designed piece of pottery that's been knocked to the floor, paradise has been shattered to smithereens. Between the "already" and the "not yet" we simply won't get, in any situation, location, or relationship, anything remotely close to the stunningly perfect beauty of paradise.

So you have a choice. You can give yourself to a constant chorus of situational and relational complaints, making sure you let God and the people around you know that you are not happy at all with the way things are. You can be critical, judgmental, and demanding, making your relationships toxic and yourself unbearable to be around. Or you can stay committed to the delusion that somehow you will find or create paradise. You will try to control what you cannot control and require what will never be delivered. You can be on the constant move, regularly leaving situations, locations, and relationships because they did not measure up, and investing in the new place, with new people, in the hope that it will deliver. You'll end up lonely, disappointed, and alienated, but you'll probably keep looking.

Now, none of these options will produce spiritual, emotional, or relational health in you, and they surely won't leave you with the restful joy of contentment. There is a third option, which the Lenten season can stimulate. How about mourning paradise lost? Jesus says something rather shocking in his Sermon on the Mount: "Blessed are those who mourn, for they shall be comforted" (Matt. 5:4). We would tend to think just the opposite: "Blessed are those who have no reason whatsoever to mourn." Jesus is speaking with a full and experiential knowledge of what sin has done to the world. He knows that the world he created is not operating as it was intended to operate. He knows that nothing right now will be like the paradise that once was. He knows the value of recognizing the damage and weeping. Imagine standing in front of your house that contained all your memories and all your possessions after it had been reduced to rubble by a tornado. Wouldn't you stand there and weep?

Jesus is standing in front of the house that he built, a world filled with beautiful things that he made, now broken to pieces by sin, and he is saying to us, "Look around. How can you not weep?" Mourning is healthy because it forces you to consider the full weight of the tragedy of sin. Mourning is healthy because it forces you to let go of the delusion that you can turn the rubble into paradise. Mourning is healthy because it makes you cry out for a restorer. Mourning is healthy because it causes you to hold tightly to God's promise of paradise to come. Mourning is healthy because it teaches you how to be content between the "already" and the "not yet." Mourning is healthy because when you mourn in this way, the God of all comfort hears your cry and comes near with comfort that is profoundly more healing than a new situation, relationship, or location could ever be.

So this Lent, put your mourning into practice and into words. Let your heart be crushed at what sin has done so your heart can be comforted by your Savior. And remember to mourn with hope, because your Lord has promised that what now is will end, and what is to come is worthy to be called paradise.

Reflection Questions ───────────────────────────────

1. What are your greatest disappointments in life, and what deeper desires do those things reveal?

2. How can you "mourn paradise lost"—what does that look like in real life?

3. How might mourning paradise lost enhance your relationship with Christ?

The best way to deal with the inevitable disappointment of life here on earth is to look with hope toward our eternal destination—the new heavens and the new earth. Read Revelation 21:1–7 and rejoice in your salvation.

DAY 8

*It's good to be poor. It's the only
pathway to the riches of grace.*

You don't have to pay very close attention to see that our culture is obsessed with riches. We are very interested in the lives of wealthy people. We want to get behind the gated driveways, to get inside the closed doors, and to peek over the tall hedges to see what those castles look like and how the elite really live. We point out exotic cars to one another, talk about that once-in-a-lifetime expensive meal, or reminisce abut the crazy stores on the designer strip we once walked. We deny it, but we secretly want to be one of those wealthy people, because deep down we believe that this just may be the good life. We don't admit it to one another, but our discontent is just below the surface. We still tend to think, "If I just had _____, then I would be happy."

As Christians, we tend to esteem the spiritually rich as well. These are people who we think have risen above the normal things that we all tend to struggle with, who seem somehow to be easily and independently righteous and just don't seem to require God's rescue much. We envy people who don't seem to have any marriage struggles or who seem to parent with ease. We want to be that rich brand of Christian, you know, the kind who tends to think, desire, and do the right thing seemingly all the time.

This is where the season of Lent stops us, interrupts us, confronts us, and calls us to buy into a completely different narrative. That narrative is found in a few simple words of Jesus: "Blessed are the poor in spirit, for theirs is the kingdom of heaven" (Matt. 5:3). What? How is poverty of any kind a blessing? How is it ever good to have nothing, and to have to admit you have nothing? How is it possible for the impoverished life to be the good life? These are the questions the season of Lent forces us to face and to answer because Lent isn't for the rich; it is for those who are poor.

When Jesus says, "Blessed are the poor in spirit," he knows his words aren't as radical as they sound. Let me unpack the logic here. Jesus knows that no one is independently rich in spirit. No one independently has his act together. No one is righteous on his own. No one loves as he should in his own strength. No one naturally has all the right motives. No one's mind is independently pure. Independent spiritual riches are a delusion. People who think they are righteous are doomed. People who have successfully convinced themselves that they are okay are in trouble. People who strut their spiritual knowledge and good deeds are the ones we should be concerned for. They have bought into the darkest of delusions, that it is possible for a human being, without external intervention, to please God. Apart from the miracle of intervening, rescuing, forgiving, and transforming grace, there simply are no spiritually rich people out there, none. But self-righteousness is a self-supporting deceit. Every moment of self-assessment just deepens the blindness.

So we all need bankruptcy. This is the first step of God's work of grace in our lives. In an act of divine mercy, God opens the well-guarded vault of our righteousness to show us that, contrary to what we thought, it is absolutely empty. We then must face the shocking realization of our complete poverty, that rather than being righteous, we are, in fact, unrighteous in every way, and this drives us to cry out for forgiveness and help. In this way the magnificent blessings of the kingdom of God are open and available only to the poor. It is admitting that you have nothing that causes you to reach out for the amazing "something" that is offered to you in the person and work of the Lord Jesus Christ.

Here is the whole gospel story in one verse: "You know the grace of our Lord Jesus Christ, that though he was rich, yet for your sake he became poor, so that you by his poverty might become rich" (2 Cor. 8:9). The infinitely rich one was willing to become sacrificially poor, so that we might be rescued from our bankruptcy and become rich. If there were such a thing as independently spiritually rich people, this gospel narrative wouldn't make any sense. But everyone is born poor. The only difference between us is that some of us have been given eyes to see and confess our poverty, and the rest of us are under the sad delusion that we are rich.

It is sad to note that not only are the hallways and pathways of humanity filled with people who think they are rich, but there are churches filled with them as well. If you were financially bankrupt, you'd be in a panic. You'd spend sleepless nights wondering what in the world you were going to do; you'd be crying out for help. You would be grieved, but open and approachable. You'd eventually quit faking it and face the fact that without some kind of intervention, you are doomed. Poverty wouldn't leave you relaxed, disinterested, and rather self-assured. It would make you ashamed and afraid and ready to do something about it. Spiritual passivity and spiritual disinterest are never the result of confessing that you are spiritually poor. Only those who by grace have become willing to confess how poor they actually are daily seek and celebrate the vast storehouse of riches that are theirs because of the life, death, and resurrection of Jesus.

In this season, stop and take time to assess where you're still telling yourself that you're rich (righteous) and admit the extent of your past and present poverty, so that you can truly celebrate the once-unattainable riches that are yours, not because of what you have done, but because of what has been done for you. The richest man who ever lived became poor so that we would, because of him, be rich beyond our wildest imagination. No, I do not mean in the temporary riches of physical things, but rich in the most important way: rich in spirit.

Reflection Questions ─────────────────────────────

1. If you're being totally honest with yourself, what is the thing that fills in the blank: "If I just had _____, then I would be happy"? What does this answer reveal about your spiritual condition?

2. On a daily basis, how aware are you of your spiritual bankruptcy apart from Christ? How might you grow in this awareness, particularly during the season of Lent?

3. Would your friends characterize you as spiritually self-sufficient or as one who knows the blessing of spiritual poverty—and are you satisfied with the answer to that question?

Read Ephesians 2:1–22, and reflect on who you were before Christ and what is yours in Christ.

DAY 9

Where you point the finger of blame is where you will be convinced that the most help is needed.

I was irritated with my wife, Luella. I should have responded to her in a way that was patient and kind, but in my irritation, I said things to her that I should have never said. I was negative, picky, and self-righteous, and then I was silent. She was surprised and hurt. She was driving. I didn't look at her. The car was filled with a horribly uncomfortable silence. It was as if the oxygen had been sucked out of the air. I was silent, but my mind wasn't. In my mind a big finger of blame pointed right at her. "The whole thing is her fault," I told myself. "If she hadn't done that, then I wouldn't have gotten angry," I reasoned. "I've talked to her about this before, but she never listens. Maybe she heard me this time. Maybe after this talk, things will be different. She needs to say something; she needs to say she's sorry."

You've been in similar situations. So let's unpack it together. Because what I did was wrong, my conscience bothered me. When your conscience bothers you, there are only two ways to ease it. You can point the finger of blame at yourself, confess your sin, rest in the forgiving grace of Jesus, cry out for his empowering help, and then seek the forgiveness of the person you sinned against. Having done this, you walk away with both a conscience that is clear and a reconciled relationship. Or you can point the finger of blame at the other person, denying your own responsibility and convincing yourself that he not only wronged you but that he is the cause of any wrong that you did. As you do this, your sense of offense grows, and because it does, your anger grows, as does your belief that this person simply needs to change. You are not at ease, you are riled up, and your relationship with the other person remains unreconciled.

Where you point the finger of blame will always inform you where change needs to take place. Someone once said that you never see a person in a protest carrying a sign with an arrow pointing downward and with the words "I am the problem" painted on it. One of the most significant aspects of the deceitfulness of sin is our ability to swindle ourselves into thinking that we are seldom at fault. And because we are good at convincing ourselves that we are not at fault, we also become skilled at causing ourselves to feel good about thoughts, desires, words, and actions that God says are not good. One of the ways that we tend to trouble our own trouble is our ability to convince ourselves that our sin is not so sinful after all. When you convince yourself that your sin is not so sinful after all, you also convince yourself that you don't need God's amazing, rescuing, forgiving, and transforming grace. Anyone who argues against his own need of grace is in grave spiritual danger.

Listen to what John says: "If we say we have no sin, we deceive ourselves, and the truth is not in us. If we confess our sins, he is faithful and just to forgive us our sins and to cleanse us from all unrighteousness. If we say we have not sinned, we make him a liar, and his word is not in us" (1 John 1:8–10). These are strong words, but we all need to hear and consider them. It is humbling to say what I am about to say, but I know it is true. No one has lied to me more often than I have. No one has twisted events for his advantage more than I have for myself. No one has worked harder to make me feel good about what is not good than I have. Sadly, I have often participated in my own deceit. When I do this, I feel righteous in situations where what I did was not righteous, and because I feel right, I don't seek God's forgiveness or his help. John is addressing a spiritual dynamic that operates at times in us all.

When you do what is wrong, you either look for someone to blame or you admit blame and run in humility and grief to your Redeemer. We are tempted to believe that our greatest problems in life exist outside of us. It's our husband or wife, it's that nasty neighbor, it's our children, it's our boss or coworkers, it's the way women dress, it's this materialistic culture, it's our church, and, if you have nothing else to blame, it's the dog! This not only keeps you from seeking the grace and getting the help you need, but it argues against what God says is true about you. It places you in a spiritually debilitating standoff with your Redeemer. Either he is a liar, or you are. Self-deception never goes anywhere good; it never produces good fruit in your life or in your relationship with God or others. Humble, honest, specific, heart-felt confession is the doorway to peace within yourself, peace with God, peace with your neighbor, and a life of ongoing growth and fruitfulness.

Where do you tend to point the finger of blame? The gospel forces you to admit that your biggest problems in life exist inside you and not outside you, and because this is true, you need more than situational, relational, or location change.

Lent is all about pointing the finger in the right direction. It is about humble self-examination, honest confession, and grief over sin that causes you to seek and celebrate the grace Jesus was willing to suffer and die for. Because this is a season of mournful personal confession, it can also be for you a season of spiritual renewal and rejoicing. Renewal happens because confession causes you to see things as they really are, and in doing so, to begin to confess and address things that have long needed to be confessed and addressed. The more you see your sin, the more you will respond tenderly to other sinners and want for them the same grace you have received. And as you taste new life, you will begin to celebrate, in fresh new ways, the grace that is yours in Christ Jesus.

Reflection Questions

1. Think back to the last disagreement you had with someone close to you. Where did you point the finger of blame? When you were able to calm down and assess the situation rightly, were you able to identify any part you played in the conflict?

2. How have you seen the truth that "no one has lied to me more often than I have" play out in your life in the past week? What kinds of things have you justified, and what does that tell you about patterns of temptation and sin in your life?

3. In the coming days, how might you engage in personal confession in a way that brings about spiritual renewal?

Read 1 John 1:5–2:6, and spend some time in honest self-assessment, confession, and repentance.

DAY 10

*Jesus did what he did for us because
there simply was no other way.*

I think all of us can relate to finding ourselves in a mess of some kind and looking for the easy way out. We tend to buy into the hope of quick solutions with minor consequences. We hope that we can avoid personal responsibility, loss, and the cost of restoration. We can look at something that is hopelessly broken and fantasize that it's not. Or we can hope that the person who has been deeply hurt by us will let it pass this time. Or we keep banking on the hope that the physical pain we've been experiencing will just fade away. We spend too much, hoping that debt won't catch up with us, or that when it does, we'll find a novel way out. We park illegally, hoping that, miraculously, we'll be the person the parking police decide to show grace. We waste time, hoping we'll get it back somehow. We procrastinate, trusting that we'll be able to complete the task in a much shorter time than what originally seemed necessary.

In some way the quest of every fallen human being is to find the easy way out.

This is one of the reasons it is helpful to mark out a period of time each year to meditate on the cross of Jesus Christ. The cross is a powerful interruption to our "easy way out" thinking. It catches us up short. It confronts our vain wishes. The horrible suffering and death of the perfect Messiah, Jesus, on a criminal's cross, outside of the city on a hill of death, tells us in no uncertain terms that when it comes to humanity's deepest and inescapable problem, there is no easy way out. None. The cross calls us to quit hoping in, to stop searching for, and to give up on our belief in our ability to manufacture or stumble upon a cure. Sin brought death into the world. Sin separated us from our Creator. Sin turned us all into rebels and fools. Sin's pathway is destruction, and its endpoint is death. There are no escape routes. We can't buy our way out. We can't earn a better destiny. There is nothing we can do. We are being propelled blindly down a roadway of death. We may smile and celebrate and accumulate, but left to ourselves we have no hope. Apart from some miraculous intervention, we are doomed. There is and never has been any easy way out of this terminal disease, the one that infects us all: sin. The cross screams to us, "Stop looking elsewhere. This is the only way!"

The world offers endless promises of self-atonement, but each is a lie. The world offers endless excuses for sin, personal and corporate, but each is built on falsehood. The world offers philosophies built on proving that there is no God, so there is no moral responsibility, and therefore, no such thing as death.

The world offers scientific denials of divine origins and the afterlife. Most of us work to make ourselves think we're better off than we are and we don't desperately need what the cross tells us is essential.

The gravity of the cruelty meted out against Jesus forces this question upon us: "Did God really have to go to this extent to fix the problem of sin?" Did God really have to control all the situations, locations, personalities, machinations, institutions, and governments of earth so that history would march toward the right time and place: the birth of Jesus? Did Jesus really have to subject himself to the full range of the darkness and temptation of this fallen world? Was it really necessary for him to live a life that was spotlessly perfect in thought, desire, motive, choice, word, action, reaction, and response? Was it necessary for him to lay down concrete and empirical evidence during his life that he was not just a wise man, but in fact, the one and only Son of God? Was it really necessary for him to be mocked, spat upon, and executed in a torturous and public way? Was it necessary, at the point of his death, for graves to open and the veil separating the Holy of Holies to be spontaneously torn in two? Did he have to be put in a carefully sealed, well-guarded borrowed grave? Was it essential for him to be there for three days, certifying that he was really dead? Was it vital for him to walk out of that tomb, alive and well? Was it essential to the plan that he appear to some five hundred people after his resurrection? Was it necessary that he would ascend back to the right hand of his Father?

The answer to every one of these questions is a resounding yes! Every detail of the history of redemption was necessary. Every moment in the life of Christ was necessary. Every aspect of his suffering, death, and resurrection was necessary. It was all essential, because there was no other way to reverse the damage that sin had done or to rescue those who were held in its death grip. No novel solutions to be found, no quick fixes, and no exceptions to the rule. There was no easy way out.

Here's what Jesus said about his identity and his mission:

> Now it happened that as he was praying alone, the disciples were with him. And he asked them, "Who do the crowds say that I am?" And they answered, "John the Baptist. But others say, Elijah, and others, that one of the prophets of old has risen." Then he said to them, "But who do you say that I am?" And Peter answered, "The Christ of God."
>
> And he strictly charged and commanded them to tell this to no one, saying, "The Son of Man must suffer many things and be rejected by the elders and chief priests and scribes, and be killed, and on the third day be raised." (Luke 9:18–24)

Take time during this season to focus on the doom that was your destiny apart from the cross. Meditate on what God was willing to do in order to purchase your forgiveness, reconciliation, and new life. Think about the terminal disease that you were born with and your need for the Great Physician, the sacrificial Lamb, the suffering servant Jesus, and be thankful. And may this season of remembrance free you from ever again minimizing your sin and buying into the vain hope that there may be an easy way out.

Reflection Questions ————————————————————

1. In what ways do you look for the easy way out, spiritually speaking? Where are you making shortcuts in your walk with the Lord, and what effect do you think that is having on your life?

2. Write out the gospel in simple terms, the way you would if you were talking with an unbelieving friend. Better yet—share it with an unbelieving friend. What fresh insight do you gain from looking at the gospel with fresh eyes, as if for the first time?

3. How would you answer the question, Why was all this sacrifice really necessary?

Read Romans 5:1–21, and rejoice in Christ's finished work on your behalf.

DAY 11

*The cross of Jesus Christ purchased
more than forgiveness for you.*

We should forever celebrate the cross of Jesus Christ as the only possible means of forgiveness. That celebration should mark our lives now and for the rest of eternity. But we cannot restrict our understanding and celebration of the cross to its value as God's gracious means of forgiveness, because the cross offers us so much more. There is an aspect of what the cross provides for us that is essential to our lives as God's children that I don't think we study enough, meditate on enough, or celebrate enough.

Pretend that I had done something extremely hurtful to you, something that was a terrible betrayal of the love and trust between us, something that was a self-oriented denial of the way any healthy relationship was meant to operate. And pretend that you had confronted me, and after defending myself I confessed that what I had done was a terrible personal affront. Pretend with me that after my confession, grief flooded into my heart and I came to you with tears of sorrow and asked for your forgiveness. Pretend that you were kind and gracious and were willing to forgive me, and not only that, you were willing to reconcile with me so that we could be in friendship with one another again. And pretend that your forgiveness and our reconciliation had removed my guilt and brought peace not only between us, but in my heart. With all of the grace of forgiveness and reconciliation, there is still something I desperately need that you are not able to give me. Do you know what it is?

You could not work changes inside me that would ensure that not only would I never do the same thing again, but I would treat you with a deeper love and respect and have a fresh commitment to give and to serve. You can forgive me, but you are not able to change me. What you did for me was wonderful and kind, but because you are human and limited, it is not enough. The cross of Jesus Christ not only does the first two things for us (forgiveness and reconciliation), but it also does the third thing for us (change). Let's look at how the writer of Hebrews talks about this often neglected aspect of the transforming grace of the cross of Jesus Christ.

> But when Christ appeared as a high priest of the good things that have come, then through the greater and more perfect tent (not made with hands, that is, not of this creation) he entered once for all into the holy places, not by means of the blood of goats and calves but by means of his own blood, thus securing an eternal redemption. For if the blood of

goats and bulls, and the sprinkling of defiled persons with the ashes of a heifer, sanctify for the purification of the flesh, how much more will the blood of Christ, who through the eternal Spirit offered himself without blemish to God, purify our conscience from dead works to serve the living God. (Heb. 9:11–14)

What a power-packed statement of grace that is ours because of the cross of Jesus Christ! It would take many devotionals to explore all the glories of grace that these words lay before us. But I want to draw your attention to the final thought: "How much more will the blood of Christ . . . purify our conscience from dead works to serve the living God" (Heb. 9:14). What is the writer of Hebrews talking about, and why is it so important? To answer the question, you have to understand the vital function of the conscience in the way God designed us and intended us to live.

The conscience is the inner alarm system that God designed to warn us and redirect us. It is a beautiful thing to have a tender and lively conscience. It is beautiful when your conscience alerts you to moral danger or plagues you when you have done what is wrong. The conscience is an irreplaceable tool that God has built within us so that we would live as he intended. But sin has damaged the function of this vital tool of the heart.

In order to understand that damage, you have to understand that your alarm that is your conscience only sounds based on the standard that your heart has surrendered to. This means that a good and godly moral value system will allow your conscience to function properly, but a bad and self-centered moral value system will mean that your conscience will do you harm. Since sin causes us all to exchange worship and service of the Creator for worship and service of the creation, and since the thing that is at the center of that idolatry is ourselves, without divine intervention our consciences just don't operate the way God intended.

But there is another way that sin interrupts and distorts the work that God intended the conscience to do. The conscience is able to do its work only if it can see clearly, anticipating the moral danger ahead or focusing on a failure that has just happened. Moral sightedness is essential to the proper function of the essential tool of the heart. Here's the problem with the need for the conscience to see clearly: sin blinds. Sin causes the conscience to be unable to see what it needs to see to sound the moral alarm. And sin not only blinds the conscience so it cannot function as God intended; sin also causes the conscience to be blind to its blindness. So we think we are seeing clearly and that the alarm system is working well, but in our sin, we are trusting what is blind and what lives under an idolatrous value system to be morally trustworthy.

Hebrews tells us that the blood of Christ does this amazing thing: it cleanses the conscience. It cleanses it from its bondage to self and the surrounding creation. It cleanses it of its blindness, imparting to it a renewed ability to see. It cleanses it from a corrupt moral value system, giving room now for a life dedicated to and directed by a desire to live according to God's law and for his glory. The cross doesn't just purchase God's forgiveness for us, but it also changes us. And at the heart of that change is a conscience that has been cleansed by the transforming grace of the blood of Jesus.

Every time you see sin ahead and avoid it, and every time you look back on what you have done with moral grief, you are experiencing the grace of the cleansing of your conscience. This is a vital and precious aspect of what Jesus did on the cross for you and for me that we often neglect when we are meditating on and celebrating the death of Jesus. This Lenten season don't just reflect on the necessity of your forgiveness; take time also to consider the amazing grace of a conscience that has been cleansed and is able now more than ever before to do in you and for you what God intended.

Reflection Questions

1. What aspects of the idea that the cross offers us more than forgiveness were new to you?

2. When was the last time your conscience kicked in and prevented you from doing something you knew you shouldn't do? Would you characterize your conscience as tender or damaged?

3. What are some things you can do to help yourself be more sensitive to your conscience?

Read Romans 2:1–16, and ask the Lord to convict you of any sin you have been ignoring.

DAY 12

Your emotional life is a window into what is truly important to you and what you are really living for.

It bothered me more than I was willing to admit. It made me angry. It made me fearful. It discouraged me again and again. As much as I tried to ignore it, it would hook me again. I could argue that it didn't make any difference at all, but it was important to me and I could not escape my struggle. It would sneak up on me and grab me unexpectedly, and it would distract and divert me. It hurt, and the hurt would not go away. One man's approval had become my god.

I was a young pastor who was learning his way. Of course there were moments when my leadership was awkward. I'm sure at times I thought I knew more and was capable of more than I actually was. I'm sure at that time I was not a very good preacher. If this particular person was intent on criticizing me, I gave him plenty of material to work with. But change began to take place when I began to understand that he was not my problem; I was. It was a bit mortifying to confess that I had put this man in a position in my life that only God should be in. I had allowed him to do for me what only God could do. This man had the power to wreck not just a day for me but an entire week as I hashed over and over in my mind another situation of his dismissal. My heart had wandered away from trusting in God and the rest of heart that is found in hooking your identity and security to him.

What alerted me to the fact that the problem was me? The answer is not mysterious or complicated: it was my emotions. I had every reason to be joyful. I had been chosen and gifted to be a minister of the gospel of Jesus Christ. I had a wonderful wife and the beginnings of a beautiful family. Our little church was becoming a close-knit gospel community that felt more like a family than an institution. The Lord was meeting our physical needs. In many ways these were some of the best years of our lives, but I was discouraged, fearful, anxious, doubtful, and ill at ease. I had lost the confidence that I once had in the gifts God had given me and his calling to this particular place of ministry. In my discouragement I spent way too much time contemplating what it would be like to not be a pastor anymore. The thought of continuing made my stomach churn, while the thought of leaving gave me hope. I was a mess.

Our emotions are a window into what our hearts really love. The rise and fall of your feelings function as a barometer to what you truly value and want out of life. Your joy, sadness, fear, anger, happiness, despondency, contentment, discouragement, rejoicing, and inner grumbling can point you to what is ruling your heart at street level. When the Bible commands you to rejoice, it is calling you to surrender the control of your heart to the one who always gives you reason to rejoice, no matter what is going on in your life. Circumstantial, relational, and experiential joy is always temporary, because the "good" moments those things give us are temporary. Lack of peace may indicate that where you have looked for peace will never deliver the peace you crave. Fleeting happiness may indicate that you've hooked your happiness to something that wasn't created to give you lasting happiness. Fear may indicate you have trusted something that is fallen and broken and will never faithfully deliver what you are looking for. Discouragement may point you to the fact that you keep hoping in something in your world, and that thing keeps failing you because it was not meant to supply you with unbroken hope.

Here's the bottom line. Your emotions can be a helpful indicator of where you have replaced God with something else or where you have asked him to deliver to you something he's never promised. Often we make the mistake of thinking we have a heart for the Lord, when really we're just thankful for him because at that moment he seems to be delivering to us what we have truly set our hearts on. Often we reduce God to just the deliverer of good gifts, rather than recognizing him as the ultimate heart-satisfying gift.

In this fallen world we all face a catalog of potential God replacements. The list is endless because anything in creation can capture our hearts and live there as only God should. As a young pastor, the respect of one man was that God-replacement for me. I was a pastor; I was studying the Bible or teaching, preaching, or counseling the Bible all the time. I spent much of my life thinking about God and his word. I talked all the time about the liberating joy of following him and the dangers of sin. I thought I was, on the inside, a God-fearer and a willing servant. But there was evidence that something was amiss. I had none of the peace and rest of heart that communion with the Lord should produce. I had just the opposite, because although I thought of myself as serving God, I was in active service of a false god, and my emotional life was the evidence that began to help me to see what was going on beneath the surface of my seemingly Godward life.

In this season of reflection, confession, and willing sacrifice, how about scanning the evidence in your own life? How about taking stock of what your emotions tell you about what you're truly serving? How about being willing to confess to having a fickle and wandering heart? How about not assuming that the habits of religion mean that your heart is ruled by the Lord at street level? How about offering to God the one sacrifice he will never reject, the sacrifice of humble, honest, heartfelt confession? Remember David's words of assurance to all who would come to God and confess a wandering heart: "The sacrifices of God are a broken spirit; / a broken and contrite heart, O God, you will not despise" (Ps. 51:17). You are never in a safer, more blessed place than when your heart is broken in this way.

Reflection Questions ————————————————————

1. What is your current emotional state? Is there a negative emotion that is present in your life more often than it should be?

2. If "our emotions are a window into what our hearts really love," what do your emotions say about what you love?

3. Think about the spiritual habits you engage in, perhaps even your devotional times—are you covering up sins or idols with religious practice?

Read Colossians 3:1–10. Ask yourself if your focus is on things above, or if the negative actions and attitudes listed are present in your life, revealing a focus on the things of earth.

DAY 13

*Every piece of Christ's suffering was suffered for you,
and every victory accomplished by that suffering was
accomplished so that you can now live in victory too.*

Whatever inconvenience or temporary suffering we may endure during Lent, as we withhold things from ourselves in order to focus on the gravity of our sin and the glory of God's redeeming plan, it is infinitesimal in comparison to what Jesus willingly endured as our substitute. Now, I know the term *substitute* today sometimes implies inadequacy. But the substitutionary function of everything Christ did is one of the chief glories of his work on earth. We think of substitutes as being inadequate when compared to the one they are standing in for, but the opposite is true in the case of the second Adam, Jesus. In this case, *the substitute is marvelously greater*. Let me explain.

1. Jesus was the substitute for Adam and Eve. Because the first Adam failed, there was a crying need for a second Adam who would obey God in every way in every situation, location, and relationship, each and every time. The Messiah Jesus would be Adam's substitute, doing, with complete perfection, what Adam failed to do. But he came to be not only Adam's substitute, but yours and mine as well. Because of sin, everyone would fall short of God's standard, so no one would be able to earn God's acceptance based on his or her keeping of the law. God's righteous requirement was fully satisfied in the perfectly righteous life of Jesus. Because of the complete righteousness of the second Adam, who endured every kind of temptation, sinners like you and me can stand before a holy God and be received as righteous in his eyes. Consider how the essential grace of the perfect substitute, Jesus, is captured in Romans 5:

> Therefore, just as sin came into the world through one man, and death through sin, and so death spread to all men because all sinned—for sin indeed was in the world before the law was given, but sin is not counted where there is no law. Yet death reigned from Adam to Moses, even over those whose sinning was not like the transgression of Adam, who was a type of the one who was to come. . . .
>
> For if, because of one man's trespass, death reigned through that one man, much more will those who receive the abundance of grace and the free gift of righteousness reign in life through the one man Jesus Christ.
>
> Therefore, as one trespass led to condemnation for all men, so one act of righteousness leads to justification and life for all men. For as by the one man's disobedience the many were made sinners, so by the one man's obedience the many will be made righteous. Now the law came in to increase the trespass, but where sin increased, grace abounded all the

more, so that, as sin reigned in death, grace also might reign through righteousness leading to eternal life through Jesus Christ our Lord. (Rom. 5:12–14, 17–21)

2. Jesus was the substitute for the animals of sacrifice. The reason animal after animal had to be sacrificed day after day, in an endlessly bloody scene, was because they were not an adequate payment for the penalty of sin. The animal sacrifices were God's gracious provision until the coming of the ultimate, final sacrifice of the unblemished Lamb of God, the Lord Jesus Christ. Here also Jesus stood as a substitute, doing what no animal sacrifice was ever able to do: atone for sin. Jesus, the Lamb, had to be willing to be the perfect sacrifice to end all ineffective animal sacrifices. He had to be willing to suffer and die, and because he was willing, we will never have to fear God's anger. Hebrews 10:1–10 brilliantly explains this:

> For since the law has but a shadow of the good things to come instead of the true form of these realities, it can never, by the same sacrifices that are continually offered every year, make perfect those who draw near. Otherwise, would they not have ceased to be offered, since the worshipers, having once been cleansed, would no longer have any consciousness of sins? But in these sacrifices there is a reminder of sins every year. For it is impossible for the blood of bulls and goats to take away sins.
>
> Consequently, when Christ came into the world, he said,
>
> "Sacrifices and offerings you have not desired,
>   but a body have you prepared for me;
> in burnt offerings and sin offerings
>   you have taken no pleasure.

> Then I said, 'Behold, I have come to do your will,
>> O God,
>>> as it is written of me in the scroll of the book.'"

When he said above, "You have neither desired nor taken pleasure in sacrifices and offerings and burnt offerings and sin offerings" (these are offered according to the law), then he added, "Behold, I have come to do your will." He does away with the first in order to establish the second. And by that will we have been sanctified through the offering of the body of Jesus Christ once for all.

3. Jesus was the substitute for the Old Testament priests. For all their dedicated and disciplined sacrificial and intercessory work, the priests were part of a system that was earthbound, temporary, and ultimately ineffective. Jesus came as the better priest. He was heaven-sent, his priestly work was effective and once-for-all. He was not only the perfect substitute for all those Old Testament priests, he was the sacrifice as well. As the perfect priest, he offered to God the perfect, acceptable sacrifice, himself, forever ending, by his self-sacrifice, any further need for a sacrifice for sin. Read how this is celebrated in Hebrews 7:23–28:

> The former priests were many in number, because they were prevented by death from continuing in office, but he holds his priesthood permanently, because he continues forever. Consequently, he is able to save to the uttermost those who draw near to God through him, since he always lives to make intercession for them.

For it was indeed fitting that we should have such a high priest, holy, innocent, unstained, separated from sinners, and exalted above the heavens. He has no need, like those high priests, to offer sacrifices daily, first for his own sins and then for those of the people, since he did this once for all when he offered up himself. For the law appoints men in their weakness as high priests, but the word of the oath, which came later than the law, appoints a Son who has been made perfect forever.

If Jesus willingly endured what he endured and suffered all that he suffered to be the perfect substitute, doing for you what you could have never done for yourself, would you not be willing to make sacrifices for him? "I appeal to you therefore, brothers, by the mercies of God, to present your bodies as a living sacrifice, holy and acceptable to God" (Rom. 12:1). May God give you the grace to do just that. Do you find comfort attractive and sacrifice hard? Perhaps your first sacrifice this Lenten season should be a sacrifice of confession, admitting your struggle to let go of the world in order to hold more tightly to your Lord.

Reflection Questions

1. Have you given something up for Lent? How is it going? What sacrifices are hardest for you to make, and why do you think those particular things are so hard for you to give up?

2. How does the fact that Jesus was the perfect second Adam impact your salvation and your daily life?

3. How does it impact your life that Jesus is your substitute sacrifice and your substitute high priest? How can you more intentionally celebrate these wonderful truths?

Read Isaiah 53:1–12, and meditate on the list of sacrifices Jesus bore for you.

DAY 14

*One of the scariest, most destructive aspects of sin is its
ability not only to blind us, but to blind us to our blindness.*

I fell into the trap once again. I didn't see it coming, and I didn't
know it was happening until after the fact. I am sure I am not
alone in this. I am persuaded it happens to us more often than
we realize. It makes us closed, self-protective, and defensive. It
prevents us from learning and growing. It weakens our receptivity
to preaching and the ministry of the body of Christ. It makes us
rather hard to live with and unapproachable. I was tempted once
again to believe something that is not true, to accept it unchal-
lenged, and to act upon it. It didn't go well in the moment, and
it would have done me harm if God hadn't met me by his grace
and opened my eyes.

A dear friend asked to see me, and when we met, he confronted
me about my attitude in an email conversation. I was defensive,
because I fell into the trap that so many of us fall into. We suc-
cumb to believing that no one knows us better than we know

ourselves. There is no more dangerous aspect of sin's deceitfulness than this one. It will close you off from the insight-giving ministry of God's word, it will cause you to resist divine conviction, and it will shut you off from the essential sanctifying ministry of the body of Christ. There is no more destructive delusion than this one.

You see, if sin blinds—and it does (see Heb. 3:12–13)—then I will not have an accurate view of myself as long as there is sin remaining in me. The remaining deceitfulness creates pockets of personal spiritual blindness that will result in functional inaccuracies in the way I see, examine, and assess myself. This results in thinking I am more righteous, mature, consistent, or godly than I actually am, because there is sin of thought, desire, attitude, word, or action that I do not see or assess properly.

Now, if I think that no one knows me better than I know myself, and you come to me confronting me with something that I haven't seen, I feel no guilt in rejecting what you have to say about me. In fact, I will feel hurt that you have misjudged me in this way. Rather than feeling loved by you and by God and helped by you and God to grow in insight and maturity, I will feel wrongly condemned. Your ministry to me, rather than being hope-giving, will be seen as an affront, and if this happens repeatedly, well, there won't be much relationship left between us. I will walk away thinking that wrongful accusations ended our relationship, when really, you were attempting to do for me exactly what I and everyone else need.

All this happens because sin not only blinds us, but it also blinds us to our blindness. We think we see clearly, when we don't. We think we know ourselves, when in fact, we don't know ourselves as well as we think we do. We think that we're open to God and to the ministry of others, when we can be way more defensive than we realize. We think we are approachable, but we get quickly argumentative when we are accused of something that is outside the field of our own self-knowledge. We fall easily into this attractive trap of delusion, assuming that we know ourselves better than anyone else does or ever will.

Today there will be thousands and thousands of conversations that become awkward, uncomfortable, and derailed because of what I have just described. Many of us resist the loving, correcting, and protecting convicting ministry of the Holy Spirit, but we do not know it. Many of us say we love the church, but we are functionally not open, not approachable, and not humbly ready to listen when we are confronted by what we have not seen or do not know about ourselves. So I want to encourage you to do some new things during this Lenten season.

1. Take some time to confess your blindness, and pray for grace to see.

2. Admit to God and others that there have been times when you have been less than open and approachable.

3. Forsake forever the belief that no one knows you better than yourself.

4. Pray for the willingness to benefit from the confronting love of others.

5. Go to the principal people in your life, and ask them to help you to see what you probably wouldn't see without them.

6. Take time to celebrate that your Savior of grace won't leave you to your blindness now, and that the day is coming when your blindness will forever end.

Reflection Questions ————————————————————

1. Do you believe that you know yourself better than anyone else does? When have you seen that this might not be the case?

2. Think back on a time when you were hardened toward your sin or distant from God. At that time, were there sins you were not admitting to yourself?

3. Ask a close friend if there are areas of hardheartedness or sins that he or she has noticed you are becoming blind to. Be humbly, prayerfully ready to receive the answer with gratitude and grace.

Read Psalm 139, where we learn about God searching our hearts and knowing us even when we are misjudged by others. Ask God to search your heart, and confess any sin he reveals to you.

DAY 15

*The core enemy in our struggle with sin is not wrong
behavior, but the idolatry behind the behavior.*

The God of grace has given us an interesting passage in the
book of Ezekiel so that we would have a clearer understanding of the nature of our daily battle with sin. Because I'm convinced that on this side of eternity, life is one big spiritual war,
I have gone back to this passage again and again. Spiritual war
is what makes marriage and parenting difficult. Spiritual war is
what messes up our friendships and causes us to get ourselves into
hopeless debt. Spiritual war causes us to eat too much and to go
to places on the internet we should not go. Spiritual war makes it
easy for us to blow three hours binge-watching a series on Netflix,
while the same amount of time spent studying God's word seems
so hard. Spiritual war causes us to be materialistic, entitled, and
demanding, never quite satisfied and never truly happy. Spiritual
war is at the root of endless human disappointment and heartache.
We are all in a war, whether we know it or not.

If you want to understand your spiritual battles, you need to know and understand Ezekiel 14:1–5:

> Then certain of the elders of Israel came to me and sat before me. And the word of the LORD came to me: "Son of man, these men have taken their idols into their hearts, and set the stumbling block of their iniquity before their faces. Should I indeed let myself be consulted by them? Therefore speak to them and say to them, Thus says the Lord GOD: Any one of the house of Israel who takes his idols into his heart and sets the stumbling block of his iniquity before his face, and yet comes to the prophet, I the LORD will answer him as he comes with the multitude of his idols, that I may lay hold of the hearts of the house of Israel, who are all estranged from me through their idols.

In order to understand this convicting and illuminating passage, we must understand two terms. The first is *stumbling block*. In the Bible a stumbling block is anything or anyone that leads you to desire to do something that is wrong in the eyes of God (sin). The second term is *idol*. The biblical teaching on idolatry goes way beyond the sphere of formal religious idolatry. It's possible that you can have no formal religious idols in your life and yet be serving idols every day. Here's how the Bible defines idolatry: an idol is any person, place, or thing that exercises control over the thoughts and desires of your heart that only God should have.

At first look, this passage is about the right people doing the right thing. The elders of Israel, who are the nation's spiritual leaders, are coming to God's prophet to hear a word from the

Lord. But the message that came back was not at all what they expected to hear. God essentially says, "These men have idols in their hearts that will put a wicked stumbling block before their faces, and because this is true, it is the only thing that I am interested in talking about." God is saying that whatever rules your heart will exercise inescapable control over your behavior. Whatever captures your thoughts and desires will then direct the things that you do and say. God knew that if he did not deal with the deeper issue of their idolatry, whatever he told them would be twisted by or used in service of their idols. Notice that God is not talking about statues of false gods, but something that had taken residence in and control over the hearts of these men.

You can be theologically aware and biblically literate and still be serving idols in your daily life. You can be faithful in personal daily worship and still have actions, reactions, and responses at street level that are shaped by idols. You can be involved with ministry and have areas in your life that are under the active and functional control of something other than God. It could be the love or respect of another person, it could be the desire for control, it could be a position of power and influence, it could be the desire for a certain experience, it could be the need to be right, or the quest to be successful, or the love of theological knowledge, or the desire for material possessions. It could be hatred or bitterness against another person, it could be physical strength or beauty, it could be anything in creation that replaces the rightful rule of the Creator in your heart. Anything this side of God can become an idol.

This is where the spiritual war rages. It always rages at the level of the thoughts and desires of your heart. It is always deeper than behavior. It is fought at the point of the thing that controls your behavior, that is, the thoughts and motives of your heart. And this war rages on in the most mundane moments of our everyday lives. It also needs to be said that idolatry is not just the desire for what God says is evil. Desire for even a good thing becomes a bad thing when that desire becomes a ruling thing. Theological knowledge is a good thing, but if being knowledgeable becomes more important than loving the one that is the object of that knowledge, theological knowledge has become an idol and will cause you to make bad choices in thought, word, and deed.

I am afraid that because of my biblical literacy, my theological knowledge, and my ministry commitments, I have sometimes thought I was spiritually safe when I was not safe, because some desire in my heart was increasingly taking control of my thoughts and shaping my words and actions.

What about you? Do you tend to think that spiritual warfare doesn't include you? Have you fallen into thinking that because of your involvement in the body of Christ and its ministries that there could be no idols in your life? Have you assumed a level of personal spiritual safety that may not be true? During this season of Lent, how about confessing to a wandering heart? How about asking your Lord to reveal to you where your heart may be under the control of something other than God? How about examining what you really crave or what you really want for your life? How about looking for that person, place, or thing that has become too important to you? And how about crying out for the rescuing grace that Jesus died to give you?

May sorrow over the idolatry that still plagues you drive you into a deeper dependency on the rescuing and forgiving grace of your Savior and into a deeper celebration of the freedom that he promises you now and even more completely in the forever with him that is to come.

Reflection Questions ───────────────────────────

1. What are the stumbling blocks in your life—those things that tempt you to sin?

2. What are the idols in your life—things that control your thoughts and desires or that you crave in an unhealthy way?

3. What are you doing to remove the stumbling blocks and idols from your heart?

Read Ephesians 6:10–18, and resolve to fight the spiritual battle for your heart with the weapons God has provided.

DAY 16

No sacrifice is more pleasing to your Lord than the sacrifice of words in the form of humble, honest, heartfelt confession.

Something inside us naturally resists confessing. It is easy for us to rise to our own defense. It is easy for us to blame someone else. It is easy to argue within ourselves that what we did was not that bad after all. It is easy to compare ourselves to others and conclude that we're not doing as badly as them. It's easy to be self-righteous and defensive when approached with a wrong. But confession is counterintuitive. Every parent knows that honest, humble confession is unnatural. If you ask your child why he did what he did, he won't talk about himself. He'll point to his sibling or he'll point to the situation, but he won't say, "It was me. I am a rebel and a sinner, and I alone am at fault."

I have an embarrassing personal example of the difficulty of confession. I was on a speaking trip and staying at the home of one of the families in the church. It was a lovely, well-decorated house, filled with fine furniture. In my room was a large and beautiful leather lounge chair. When I speak, I like my clothes to be wrinkle-free, so, before the days when I would stay in hotels where irons are provided, I always traveled with a small iron. I looked around for a place to iron my clothes, and the big leather chair seemed like the best option. I put a towel on it, heated up the iron, and began to press my clothes. I had pressed my pants, set the iron upright on the towel, and walked over to get my shirt. I turned around only to discover that the iron had fallen, had landed facedown on the seat of that chair, and had burned the leather. I couldn't believe it. I then spent way too much time thinking about how I would break the bad news of how my hosts' beautiful chair now had a large burn mark, but I spent even more time trying to convince myself that this wasn't actually my fault.

I was the only one in the room. I was the one ironing. I was the one who made the decision to iron on that beautiful chair. I had walked away and left a hot iron in a precarious position. It was my fault. I had to go downstairs and tell my host what I had done. The fact that it was so hard was a humbling spiritual lesson for me. This is why confession is such a pleasing sacrifice to your Lord. It requires you to silence all the self-aggrandizing, self-righteous voices in your life. It forces you to admit that you're way more spiritually needy than you would like to think you are. It asks you to admit that you're a person in constant need of forgiveness. It causes you to admit that your biggest problem is not your history, your family, your friends, your culture, your economic situation, your church, your neighbors, your age, or your physical condition. Confession requires you to admit that your biggest problems live inside you, in your heart. It smashes any delusion of comfortable independence. It yanks you away from spiritual self-reliance. Confession drives you to the feet of God as your sovereign Lord and Savior, to honor him for who he is, and to cry for help because of who you are. Confession is pleasing to God because it puts you right in the middle of the position you were created to be in: humble, honest dependence on him.

No passage captures this better than Hosea 14:1–3:

> Return, O Israel, to the LORD your God,
>> for you have stumbled because of your iniquity.
> Take with you words
>> and return to the LORD;
> say to him,
>> "Take away all iniquity;
> accept what is good,
>> and we will pay with bulls
>> the vows of our lips.
> Assyria shall not save us;
>> we will not ride on horses;
> and we will say no more, 'Our God,'
>> to the work of our hands.
> In you the orphan finds mercy."

Hosea is a message of exhortation and warning to people who have wandered away from God. The word picture for this warning is marital adultery. God's people have committed spiritual adultery. Spiritual adultery is loving something more than God, causing us to desire and do what God has prohibited. Sin is spiritual adultery. In the face of this, Hosea calls God's people to return, as an adulterous spouse would return to the one he promised his lifelong love to. But at the center of this call to return is this request: "Take with you words . . . 'we will pay with bulls the vows of our lips.'" It is a bit hard in the English translation to understand what is being requested here. God is saying, "There is a sacrifice I want you to make; it's the sacrifice of your lips, that is, confession." God wanted them to do more than just bring the required animal sacrifices. He wanted them to bring a far more costly sacrifice: honest, humble confession, free of excuse or blame-shifting. Confession is hard, but it is simple. Confession only takes three words: "I have sinned." Confession is naming and owning the sin with no contingencies added.

But there is another part of the sacrifice of your lips. It is acknowledging that your only hope is the forgiving and transforming grace of the Lord. "Assyria shall not save us; / we will not ride on horses; / and we will say no more, 'Our God,'/ to the work of our hands. / In you the orphan finds mercy" (Hos. 14:3). Sin is a mess we cannot independently get ourselves out of. Sin cries out for grace because grace is the sinner's only hope in life and in death.

So this Lenten season, don't just give up physical stuff. How about coming to God with the pleasing sacrifice of confession? Come to him this season and place your pride on his altar, confessing your wandering heart and acknowledging once again that you are a person in need of mercy, and the mercy you need is found only in him.

In this season of sacrifice, take words with you and return to your Lord.

Reflection Questions ——————————————————————

1. Why do you think confession is so difficult for us?

2. What are the essential aspects of confession? Break it down into what actually needs to be admitted and what must not be said in order for it to be a true confession.

3. Think of someone you have wronged today, or in the past week, and go to that person with a real, honest confession of your guilt.

Set a timer and spend fifteen minutes in honest confession, using Romans 3:10–18 as a guide.

DAY 17

*The Christian life is a battle of treasure. Whatever
treasure captures your heart will control your life.*

As I would walk with my children through the streets of
Philadelphia, I would tell them to keep looking down every
once in a while, because on the edge of the street at the curb there
was treasure to be found. My kids loved finding nickels and dimes
and little metal trinkets, but they fantasized about finding real
treasure. We found no diamond rings or collectable old coins,
but my children never stopped hunting and hoping for treasure.

Every human being is a treasure hunter. We're all looking for
that thing of value that will give us life, or at least change our
lives. So we hunt for treasure in relationships, careers, possessions, achievements, education, positions of power, or in physical
strength and beauty. We never seem to find that pot of heart-
satisfying gold that we're looking for, at least not in the physical,
created world. But sadly, many of us keep looking. With despera-
tion or determination, we look again and again, telling ourselves

that the next thing will deliver what it was never designed to deliver: life.

Matthew 6 reminds us that there are only two places to look. You can attach the desires of your heart and the hope of your life to earthbound treasure or heavenward treasure. You are searching horizontally or looking vertically for that thing of such rare and amazing value that it would have the power to finally satisfy your heart and give you meaning, purpose, and security for the rest of your life. What people fail to realize is that they are searching not for a thing, but for a person. The search for treasure is, in reality, a search for a savior. This is why where you look is so terribly important. Millions and millions of people every day surrender the hope of their hearts to false saviors. They look to the created thing to do what only the Creator can. This vain search that somehow captures us all began with Adam and Eve when they looked for life away from God toward something else. Where you look for treasure will not only control your heart, and therefore, your words and behavior, but it will also determine your destiny. Treasure decisions have huge consequences here and now and in the life that is to come.

Listen to this parable of Jesus found in Matthew 13:44: "The kingdom of heaven is like treasure hidden in a field, which a man found and covered up. Then in his joy he goes and sells all that he has and buys that field."

This is the kind of story that excites us all, the kind that makes you say to yourself, "I wish I were that guy!" He found what we're all looking for, and he is so filled with joy that he has no problem whatsoever in selling everything he has so he can be certain that this treasure will be his. It's a story that's meant to stop you in your tracks, to get your attention, and to capture your imagination.

But I want you to think about something. We're all that man. We're all traversing the fields of life, and we all have our heads down looking for something that will give us hope, something that will fix what is broken in and around us, something that will satisfy our hearts. We're all looking for that thing that is worth all of the sacrifices we have made for it. Whether we know it or not, we're all searching for the one thing that we would sacrifice everything for, with no buyer's regret and no fear that we would ever wonder if we had made the wrong choice.

We all make sacrifices every day for things that we think are valuable, things that we think will carry our happiness, satisfaction, and joy. No one lives a sacrifice-free life. We give up things all the time in the hopes of possessing and experiencing something better. You can't be a human being, with the treasure orientation that is wired inside us all, and not do this. How many men have sacrificed their family for the hope of business and career success? How many teenagers have suspended their morals for the hope of the acceptance of their peers? How many politicians have dealt away their allegiance to their electorate for the hope of political power? How many people make financial and relational sacrifices to win bigger houses and better cars?

Every day we all make sacrifices for treasures that we have placed our hope in. If I could have a window into a month of your life, what sacrifices would I see you making? What would I conclude is the field that you are willing to give up precious things for? This story is not designed just to get your attention;

it is also designed to cause you to ask one of the most important questions of all: "What am I really living for?" Resist giving the "right" answer here. Regular church attendance, regular giving, along with episodes of ministry can sadly live right alongside a heart that is captured by and shaped by the sacrificial pursuit of earthbound treasure. What really does give you joy? What gets you out of bed in the morning? What has made you so content that you're not only willing to make huge sacrifices for it, but you're so satisfied you don't have the desire to search anymore? What captures the imagination and desires of your heart? You are making sacrifices, but in what field and for what treasure?

This thirty-four-word parable is meant not just to get your attention or to cause you to ask deeply personal questions, but also to confront you with a truth that every human being needs to hear and understand. The only thing that is worth sacrificing everything for is the kingdom of heaven. That kingdom is not a place or an earthly political reality. No, it is the rule of the King of kings. He comes not only to rule our hearts, but to rule over everything for our good and his glory. In his rule is the grace of forgiveness, the patient love of personal transformation, and the sovereign guarantee of life to come that is free of all the sin and suffering that so mars the here and now. His rule is the place where I am freed from my bondage to the created thing and swept up into the transcendent and glorious. This King alone is able to satisfy the cravings of my heart and grant me joy that the disappointing circumstances of life cannot take away. It really is true: the kingdom of heaven is the only thing worth giving up everything for.

So in this season of quiet spiritual reflection, stop and pay attention, ask deeply personal questions, and make a treasure evaluation. Be willing to confess where you've placed your hope in earthbound treasure, sacrificing to get what it could never deliver. And give yourself in a new way to make sacrifices in the service of the King of kings. He never promises what he cannot deliver, and he is able to do in your heart what nothing else or no one else can do.

Reflection Questions ————————————————

1. How does the way you spend your time, money, and energy reveal what you truly treasure?

2. Looking at the objective evidence of your life, do you more highly treasure the kingdom of God or earthly things?

3. What sacrifices are you willing to make for the treasure of God's kingdom?

Read Matthew 6:19–34 and 13:44–46, and meditate on where you are setting your heart.

DAY 18

The story of our redemption is historical proof
of the unstoppable sovereignty of God.

Surprise is a normal part of life for all of us. We are greeted with mystery again and again. We get caught up short, unprepared for what is coming down the line. The redemptive story confronts us with the fact that God is not like us. He saw our need, he planned how to meet that need, and everything happened just as he planned. In the vast expanse of time, the huge company of people, and the multitude of locations that were the setting for his plan of grace, he was never surprised, never unprepared, and always in control. Christ's march to the cross reinforces for us that our rest and hope are not in our knowing, but in his ruling. The God who knows no surprises will surprise us again. But it is okay, because what we don't know, *he* knows; what we can't control, *he* controls, and because he does, we can live with mystery and surprise and not be afraid.

May the words below stimulate rest in the middle of surprise.

Surprised again.

Quiet conversation erupts into heated debate.

Surprised again.

Sickness interrupts well-being.

Surprised again.

A loved one is unexpectedly lost.

Surprised again.

A long-trusted leader falls.

Surprised again.

An unexpected gift alleviates need.

Surprised again.

Opportunity's doors open wide.

Surprised again.

A sleepless night plunders rest.

Surprised again.

Sudden conflict crushes peace.

Surprised again.

An emergency alters day's schedule.

Surprised again.

Divine provision propels a plan.

Surprised again.

Sudden mystery sows confusion.

Surprised again.

Grace proves too big to grasp.

It is the story of
my life.
I am surprised again
and again.

Surprised again,
reminded again
and again,
that I am not sovereign.
I am surprised again but not afraid.
My surprise,
my misguided expectation,
the mystery I live with,
my lack of control,
does not mean
my world,
my life,
my present,
my future,
is out of control.
I will be surprised again
and again,
but I am not afraid,
because you, Lord, are incapable of being
surprised.

Reflection Questions ————————————————————

1. Do you like surprises? Why or why not? What emotions do surprises evoke for you?

2. When has life surprised you? When has God surprised you?

3. How can a perspective on God's sovereignty help you deal with the surprises of life? What are some things you can do to live with joy and hope amid the uncertainties of life?

Read Isaiah 46:5–13, and take courage and comfort in the (sometimes surprising) sovereignty of God.

DAY 19

You and I have three problems that only the
Redeemer has the power and willingness to solve.

Have mercy on me, O God,
    according to your steadfast love;
according to your abundant mercy
    blot out my transgressions.
Wash me thoroughly from my iniquity,
    and cleanse me from my sin!
For I know my transgressions,
    and my sin is ever before me.
Against you, you only, have I sinned
    and done what is evil in your sight,
so that you may be justified in your words
    and blameless in your judgment.
Behold, I was brought forth in iniquity,
    and in sin did my mother conceive me.
Behold, you delight in truth in the inward being,
    and you teach me wisdom in the secret heart.

Purge me with hyssop, and I shall be clean;
   wash me, and I shall be whiter than snow.
Let me hear joy and gladness;
   let the bones that you have broken rejoice.
Hide your face from my sins,
   and blot out all my iniquities.
Create in me a clean heart, O God,
   and renew a right spirit within me.
Cast me not away from your presence,
   and take not your Holy Spirit from me.
Restore to me the joy of your salvation,
   and uphold me with a willing spirit
Then I will teach transgressors your ways,
   and sinners will return to you.
Deliver me from bloodguiltiness, O God,
   O God of my salvation,
   and my tongue will sing aloud of your righteousness.
O Lord, open my lips,
   and my mouth will declare your praise.
For you will not delight in sacrifice, or I would give it;
   you will not be pleased with a burnt offering.
The sacrifices of God are a broken spirit;
   a broken and contrite heart, O God, you will not
      despise. (Ps. 51:1–17)

Psalm 51 records one of the most important prayers in the entire Bible. It is a prayer that everyone should emulate, because it is a model of the heart of true confession. King David, a chosen servant of the Lord, had used his position, power, and resources not only to take another man's wife, but to murder that man as well. It unpacks for us the kind of confession that comes from a truly sorrowful heart.

You see the character of this confession from the very first verse. David immediately acknowledges that his problem is not simply this occasion of sin, but something larger and more deeply serious than that. How do we know this? We know this because of the three words David uses to describe what he is dealing with: *transgression*, *iniquity*, and *sin*. These words are not synonyms but careful descriptions of the different aspects of the nature of sin. Sin is a trifold problem, not just an occasion of wrongdoing. Let's examine these together.

1. Transgression. Sin is much more than a moment of weakness that leads to doing what is wrong in the eyes of God. Surely, we all have those moments. But *transgression* concerns something deep inside us that makes us susceptible to temptation's draw and that weakens us in our battle with sin. A transgression is a willful stepping over of God's boundaries. Transgression is seeing the No Trespassing sign and climbing the fence anyway because there is something you want to get to on the other side. Transgressing is intentionally parking in the No Parking zone because you would rather save a few steps than obey the law. Transgression is yelling at your wife when you know it is wrong, because there is something that you want from her and you will do whatever is necessary to get it. Transgression is pilfering pens from work when you know very well that they weren't supplied for your personal use.

Transgression is a spirit of rebellion. It's putting yourself in God's place and writing your own rules. It's wanting your own way more than submitting to God's way. Transgression is a condition of the heart that turns every sinner into a rebel in some way. True confession confesses to more than weakness; it confesses to the rebellion of heart that causes you to be weak in your struggle with sin.

2. Iniquity. Something even deeper than a spirit of rebellion lives in me. It is the thing that causes me to be rebellious. Consider the words of Titus 1:15: "To the pure, all things are pure, but to the defiled and unbelieving, nothing is pure; but both their minds and their consciences are defiled." The only way we would ever perfectly obey God is if the thoughts, motives, desires, and intentions of our hearts were completely pure. But sin defiles the heart. Iniquity is moral uncleanness. It is like water that is no longer pure, but has corrupting elements in it. Iniquity is like breathing polluted air. You can't see it, you don't realize it, but it contains impurities that will harm you.

I wish I could say that my heart is pure. I wish I could say that there are no artifacts of moral corruption in me, and because there aren't, I am impervious to temptation. But sadly, I cannot say that, and neither can you as long as sin still resides in your heart. So confession doesn't just admit to a moment of wrongdoing and a spirit of rebellion, but it also acknowledges the moral impurity of heart that is the seedbed of that rebellion.

3. Sin. Finally, our confession of sin is a confession of a specific instance of weakness and failure. The word *sin* connotes falling short of God's wise and righteous standard. It's more than pulling the bowstring back and missing the target. It is pulling the bowstring back again and again and every time falling short of the target. Confession of a specific sin against God and others is an admission of weakness. It is an admission that, when left on our own, even in our best moments we would still fall short of God's holy requirements of us. Embedded in the word *sin* is a cry for help. It is a cry to be rescued from your bondage to yourself. It's a plea to not be left to your own weakness, but to be forgiven and recued by one greater and more powerful than you will ever be. Confession of sin carries with it a commitment to be ever more dependent on the Redeemer for the help that he alone can give. Confession of sin is an admission that this instance of weakness and failure stands as a testament of your ongoing need for God's grace.

So in this season of personal reflection and confession, may your confession be as deep and broad as David's. And may these three biblical words, *transgression*, *iniquity*, and *sin*, guide that confession. And as you confess, may you be comforted by God's promise that he will never turn his back on you. He will never despise one who comes to him with a truly broken and contrite heart. Confession is God's welcome to enter into a deeper experience of the majesty of his grace.

Reflection Questions ───────────────────────────

1. In the last week, how have you transgressed God's law, rebelling in spirit against him?

2. When was the last time you confessed your iniquity, your general impurity? If this is not a regular part of your prayer life, how might you incorporate it more often?

3. Does your confession of sin often feel like a cry for help? Why or why not?

Return to Psalm 51, and use it again as a template for prayer, allowing the definitions of transgression, iniquity, and sin to deepen your time of confession.

DAY 20

It is good to silence complaint in your life by sitting
down and taking the time to count your blessings.

So many blessings,
so many graces,
so many gifts,
so much love.
There is no rational explanation;
there is no human reason;
there is no scientific formula;
no evolutionary theory;
no political machinations;
no cultural privilege;
no chance;
no fate;
nothing earned;
nothing achieved;
nothing deserved;
no right;

no entitlement;
no family inheritance;
no right of passage;
no reward for work done;
no prize for achievement;
no deserved recognition.
There is a miracle operating here;
there is amazing favor;
there is unprecedented mercy;
there is boundless love;
there is only one explanation;
there is but one rationale.
Blood was shed
outside the city walls,
a perfect man with the criminal element
nailed to a torture tree,
hung there by those he made.
No words of defense,
no actions of resistance.
Favored Son,
now willing sufferer,
carrying the sin of multitudes.
Mocked by onlookers,
forsaken by the Father,
willing Lamb, acceptable sacrifice,
planned from eternity,
accomplished in time,
so I would know
so many blessings,

so many graces,

so many gifts,

so much love.

During this season when you are thinking about the hold that the world still has on you, when you're confessing your struggle with sin, and when you're focusing on the suffering and sacrifice of Jesus that secured your hope in this life and the one to come, take time to count the many right-here, right-now blessings that the work of Jesus has delivered to you. You probably don't need me to tell you this, but I will: it is more natural for sinners to complain than to give thanks. If you listen to yourself, you'll find that this is true. Our tendency to complain is one of the results of the selfishness of sin. Complaint reminds us that we keep sticking ourselves in the center of our worlds and making life all about us.

Gratitude is a powerful weapon against complaint. It is impossible to give thanks and complain at the same time. The more you spend time counting your blessings, the less time you'll have to number your complaints. Complaint is a distorted and inaccurate way of looking at your life. For the child of God, a life of grumbling is the result of a factually inaccurate way of assessing life. It is factually inaccurate because it misses the ultimate facts of your existence: the intervention, operation, and generous blessings of God's amazing grace. It focuses on what you don't have and forgets the marvelous blessings that are yours that you could have never earned, achieved, or deserved in your own strength or based on your own performance. God's grace unleashes into your life blessings that are too many to number. No matter what difficulties you are facing, they are outweighed by the storehouse of blessings that are yours in Christ Jesus.

So take time out of each day, if only for a few moments, to count your blessings. Buy a journal or open a Google Doc, and each day catalog the blessings in your life, from the smallest and most mundane to those that are huge and life-changing. Fight the battle with complaint by developing a day-by-day habit of gratitude. Begin counting your blessings, and watch how the practice begins to alter the way you look at your life. No one is more worthy of your praise than your generous, loving, faithful, wise, and gracious Savior.

Gratitude silences complaint.

Reflection Questions

1. Looking at a typical day, what percentage of your time is spent grumbling and what percentage is spent giving thanks?

2. Why do you think it is so difficult for us to remember to give thanks? What practical things can you do to draw your heart away from complaining and toward praise?

3. Have you ever kept a gratitude journal? What benefits did this have—or could it have if you haven't tried it yet—for you?

Read Psalm 103, and thank the Lord for his many blessings.

DAY 21

*It is impossible to excuse, deny, or minimize
your sin without telling yourself that you
do not need the grace of Christ Jesus.*

B ill and Jenny had hit the wall again. A misunderstanding had devolved into a nasty, name-calling, trust-shattering fight. The air in their house was thick with tension, and the awkward silence between them was suffocating. It had been three days since the horrible fight, but there had been no rapprochement between them. Bill spent much of those three days telling himself that Jenny was the problem, and that all he was doing was defending himself against her attack. Jenny told herself that she was the victim of an emotionally abusive husband. They could not reconcile because they were unwilling to see their own sin, let alone to confess it to God or one another. Each denied their attitudes and actions, each excused his or her sin by pointing the finger of blame at one another, and both told themselves that what they did wasn't so bad given the circumstances.

It was a familiar scene for them, repeated again and again. There was never much true confession, but somehow they would move on without the wrongs against one another being addressed and then march to the next debilitating battle. But even more tragic than the toll on their marriage was their denial of their need for the rescuing, forgiving, and empowering grace of Jesus. In refusing to confess their sin, they told themselves that they did not need the grace of Jesus, purchased for them on the cross of Calvary. Because they did not own their sin and cry out to their Savior for his forgiveness and help, they did not grow in grace and love toward one another. Their marriage was stuck in a cycle of sin and hurt. Cynicism had replaced hope, self-defensiveness had replaced trust, and a repeated cycle of hurt hardened hearts that were once tender and loving.

It makes sense that you and I simply do not reach out for help that we do not think we need. We don't long for what seems unnecessary. How is it possible to hold the cross as the epicenter of our formal theology while functionally denying our need for this radical sacrifice of love and grace? When you sin as a believer, your conscience will bother you. What you experience is the convicting grace of the Holy Spirit, and there are only four ways to respond to this gracious warning that you have done something wrong. Let's look at each response in light of what the cross requires us to see and admit about ourselves.

1. Excuse. It's hard to admit that you have done wrong, that it's your responsibility alone. It is so easy to alleviate your guilt by pointing to someone or something else as the reason you did what you did. Here's why blame-shifting seems so plausible and is so tempting. You live in a fallen world with broken things all around you, so there are many excuses to be found. You live with and near people who are less than perfect. They don't always say and do the right things. They don't always have good attitudes. They don't always keep their promises. They are not always committed to your best interest. They are just like you, people in need of God's rescuing grace.

You live with all kinds of systemic brokenness in your neighborhood, on the highways, at work, in government and education, at the stores where you shop, and the list could go on and on. In case you hadn't noticed, this is not paradise and the world doesn't function the way paradise will someday function. Yet in all of this, God meets you with his heart and life-changing, empowering grace. It really is possible to do what is right in a world that has gone wrong. This life of right begins with recognizing your need for God's grace, and that begins with a commitment to not deny your need for God's grace by searching for excuses for the wrong that you have done.

2. Deny. It is also tempting to rewrite the history of a certain situation to make yourself look way more righteous than you actually were. This may sound needlessly repetitive, but it is worth thinking about: the ultimate denial of sin is denial. Saying that it never happened makes you hopelessly unapproachable, resistant to the thought that you need to change, and self-congratulatory when you should feel guilty. It leaves you without any neediness for God's forgiving, restoring, and enabling grace. Denial never goes anywhere good, it is never good for your heart, it never deepens your relationship to God, and it never produces good in your relationships.

3. Minimize. One of the most tempting ways of escaping responsibility for your sin is not to excuse it or deny it, but to minimize it. Wrong becomes more palatable to your heart when you are able to minimize its size, importance, or impact. When you are able to make your sin look something less than a conscious moral rebellion against God or willingness to wrong your neighbor for your own good, it doesn't then feel so wrong to you. If you can make your sin look to you something less than sin, then you don't need the grace that God offers sinners. You simply cannot minimize your sin without at the same time devaluing God's amazing grace.

4. Confess. In the face of having done what is wrong in the eyes of God, this is the only option that the cross of Jesus Christ leaves open. If sin is excusable, deniable, and not really a big deal, then the cross of Jesus Christ is not necessary. Confession always recognizes the inescapable sinfulness of sin. Sin cannot be excused, it cannot be denied, and it is not honest to diminish its significance, so it must be owned and confessed to one who has the power not only to forgive, but also to deliver us from its hold on our hearts.

What is confession? Confession is admitting personal responsibility for your words and actions, without excuse of any kind or shifting the blame to anyone else. Confession is a welcome into a deeper appreciation of the presence, promises, and grace of God. It is a welcome to more humble, honest, approachable, and loving relationships with others. It is a welcome to no longer being afraid of knowing yourself or being known, because you know that nothing will ever be known or revealed about you that hasn't already been covered by the blood of Jesus. Confession is an invitation to a life of internal rest and external peace.

So this season as you reflect on the sacrifice of Christ on your behalf, and as the Spirit begins to reveal your heart and conviction sets in, don't defend yourself with excuses, denial, or minimizing, and in so doing run from the grace of your Savior. Run to him, owning what you have done as you rest in the grace he offers to all who come to him in this way. "Whoever conceals his transgressions will not prosper, / but he who confesses and forsakes them will obtain mercy" (Prov. 28:13).

Reflection Questions ———————————————

1. You probably would give verbal assent to the idea that you need God. But do your actions, your attitudes, and your prayer life support that?

2. How do you usually respond when you are confronted with your sin—excuse, deny, minimize, or confess? What factors contribute to how you respond at different times?

3. What have you noticed are the effects of each of these responses: excuse, deny, minimize, confession?

Read Psalm 62:5–8, humbling yourself in prayer before the Lord.

DAY 22

*On this side of eternity, it is easy to love
the gift more than the giver.*

Parents instinctively know that issuing warnings is an important part of true love. Parents who love their children spend a lot of time over the years warning them. From the early warnings about things that are hot, sharp, dirty, or poisonous, to the later warnings about the temptations of a fallen world, one of the ways that parents regularly express love for their children is by warning them of the dangers ahead. I have two granddaughters, and when I am with them, I find myself doing this all the time. Sometimes those warnings are attached to the rules that children have been taught and asked to obey. These warnings carry with them the threat of consequences or judgment. But warnings are not the same as judgment. If all I wanted to do was judge you, I wouldn't warn you. I warn you because I love you, and I don't want you to have to experience the consequences of your disobedience. When you are warned, you are being loved. To be warned is to receive grace.

Scripture warns us about a subtle kind of idolatry that masquerades as the worship of God but is really driven by the love of things. The war between worship of God and worship of things is not always as apparent to us as we think.

A seminary professor of mine told of a moment in his church when his brothers and sisters were enjoying a time of public praise. One woman stood up and shared how she had been facing bills that she could not pay, that she had prayed, and that God had supplied the money necessary to pay them all. Then she said, "I am just so thankful to God for his faithfulness." It seems that everything was right in this moment of praise, except my professor kept thinking, "What if he hadn't? What if God, for his eternal glory and her spiritual good, had allowed her to face the stress of the even greater financial consequences of those bills being unpaid?" Would she have still stood up and thanked God for his faithfulness?

Now, it may seem like a judgmental way of hearing this woman's gratitude, but the professor's observation points us to how subtle and deceptive the war for our hearts can be. Could it be that we are most excited about God's presence in our lives when he has met a physical need or delivered to us something that we want? Could it be that there are ways in which God has been reduced from the *one* that we love to the deliverer of the *thing* that we love? Could it be that love of the world masquerades in our hearts as the worship of God? After we get what we want and we thank God for it, we think we are worshiping him; but perhaps, in reality, what has captured our hearts is not God but a thing.

The world around us is filled with sight, sound, touch, and taste attractions. We also find delights that are not physical, like affection, success, position, respect, power, and control. All of these created things, both material and immaterial, appear to give us life. They seem to have the power to produce joy and satisfaction or, when absent, sadness and discontent. So it is quite tempting to reach for them, hoping they will do for us what they were never intended to do. It is tempting for all of us to look around and say, "If only I had _____ then my life would be _____." Whatever sits on the other side of your "if only" is the thing you are living for at that moment and the thing that you think will give you the peace of life that you think is missing.

Consider these heart-revealing questions.

When does God excite me most?

When do I shout the loudest, "God loves me!"?

When am I most thankful that I am one of God's children and the object of his fathering care?

When does my relationship with God provide me the most joy?

What does God need to do for me in order for me to be content?

When do I tend to question God's love?

When do I struggle the most to believe that God is faithful?

When am I tempted to envy others or to think God has favorites?

When does my praise of the Lord feel empty?

What causes me to feel that my prayers go unheard?

What would God have to do to produce real joy in me?

I don't know about you, but I find these questions to be uncomfortable and revealing. I don't think of myself as one who loves the gift more than the giver, but perhaps there are ways in which I do. Do I really believe that God is good, does what is good, and gives what is good to all his children all the time? Is it really true of me that because of the joy and satisfaction of knowing him and being loved by him, I am able to live with plenty or live with want? Does the withholding of what seems good cause me to question if he is good? Can I stand next to someone who has what I think I need and still love my Lord and rest in his love for me? Are there things that I have set my heart on, the absence of which will cause my faith to waver and my praise to be silenced? Where does my heart still live under the rulership of the gift rather than the righteous and loving rule of the giver?

During this season when you are letting go of the things of the world, confessing areas of sin and weakness, and running to your Savior for rescue and help, perhaps you should also confess one of the subtlest forms of idolatry. Perhaps it would be good to confess that what appears as worship may not be worship at all. It may be worship of the thing that reduces God to the delivery system for what your heart really craves. And remember, God sent his Son not only to forgive our sins, but also to liberate our hearts from the bondage to anything but him. He is not shocked or disgusted by your struggle. He will turn not away from you, but toward you with love and grace.

So today, hear this loving warning. Could it be that the confession of ongoing struggles of idolatry, no matter how subtle, is the first step toward a heart that is consumed by the worship of God alone?

Reflection Questions

1. When have you found yourself closest to God? When have you been tempted to love him for the gifts he has given rather than for himself?

2. How can you grow in your satisfaction in God himself while still being thankful for the gifts he gives?

3. What do you need to confess as an area where "what appears as worship may not be worship at all"?

Read Psalm 50:8–15, and hear God's heart of love that longs for relationship, not empty sacrifice.

DAY 23

No sacrifice that you and I will ever make is as great as the
sacrifice that was made for us and for our redemption.

Sacrifice
Everyone makes sacrifices—
for physical beauty,
for body health,
for athletic victory,
for career advancement,
for relational unity,
for sound investment,
for a physical dwelling,
for the hope of fame,
for parental love,
for spiritual growth,
for environmental health,
for political power,
for a noble cause,
for a dark addiction,

for the cause of peace,
for liberation from bondage,
for making a point,
for exposing an evil,
for meeting a need,
for offering mercy,
for settling a score,
for extending a hand.
Every day sacrifices are made.
Everyone does it.
No one can avoid it.
Life requires it.
Good calls you to it.
Evil demands it.
Sometimes we're willing.
Sometimes we're resistant.
Sometimes we regret it.
Sometimes we sacrifice with great joy,
sometimes with deep sorrow,
sometimes in the bright light,
sometimes in the darkness of night,
sometimes private,
sometimes public,
the young and the old,
men and women,
girls and boys,
of every language,
of every ethnicity,
from every place on the globe,

from every period of history.
But in all of those places,
with all of these people,
in all of those epochs of time,
with innumerable sacrifices,
there is only one man
who had sacrifice as his solitary purpose.
There was only one man
whose sacrifice would meet everyone's need.
There was only one man
who paid for what he did not do
so others would get what they did not earn.
There was only one man
who was qualified.
There was only one man
who was the God-man,
Son of God,
Son of Man.
There was only one man.
who would live a righteous life.
There was only one man
who would die an acceptable death.
There was only one man
who would satisfy God's requirement.
There was only one man
who would not only make that sacrifice
but who would be that sacrifice.
There was only one man
who would be the Lamb of God.

There was only one man
whose sacrifice would change everything.
Sin defeated.
Life given.
Hope restored.
Destiny secure.
God and man reconciled,
once for all.
"It is finished."
Billions of sacrifices made;
only one sacrifice
for life now
and for all eternity.

Reflection Questions ────────────────────────────

1. Think about the goals you're working toward right now. What are you sacrificing to reach them?

2. Does your level of sacrifice to develop your relationship with God match the level of sacrifice you make to do other things? Why or why not?

3. What sacrifice did Christ make for you? List out all that he endured, and thank him specifically for those things.

Read the account of the crucifixion in Matthew 26:20–27:53.

DAY 24

*The purpose of fasting is not to earn God's
love, but to more deeply surrender to it.*

Why would anyone ever fast? What is to be gained from giving things up? What is the purpose of not eating for a period? Why withhold from yourself what you know you're going to return to in a matter of time? Is fasting an essential spiritual discipline? Does fasting bring you closer to God? Is fasting a way to defeat sin? How do I know when to fast and what to fast from? Is there a biblical theology of fasting? How do you fast in a way that is more than a temporary denial of physical desire, but is also spiritually helpful? Does God require us to fast?

Fasting is a topic that motivates and encourages a few, but confuses many. Since Lent is a season of fasting, it is worth giving it a practical, biblical examination. My first encounter with regular and intense fasting had nothing to do with spirituality. One of my closest friends in high school was a wrestler. Because Sam was winning like crazy, there was a bit of a small town media buzz around him. He was a little guy, but he had become big man on campus, and he loved it. The problem was that he was growing fast, and his growth spurts made it hard for him to stay within the boundaries of his weight class. So Sam was always fasting. His big, luxurious meal would be Jell-O.

Although there was nothing spiritual about Sam's fast, it did have "spiritual" benefits. Because he fasted, he was more focused. Because he fasted, he became more and more committed. Because he got used to this sacrifice, other sacrifices didn't seem so hard. The pain of sacrifice brought a whole catalog of benefits to Sam and his wrestling career. I knew there was a theme of fasting in the Bible, but hanging around Sam got me thinking about the benefits of fasting as a teenager.

So why would anyone ever fast? Primarily, fasting is about focus. We all live busy lives, with so many plans and so much on our schedule. We live with constant distractions all around, and now with cell phones in our hands, there is a huge temptation to fill even the smallest quiet moment with anything. We feel compelled to keep checking Facebook, Twitter, and Instagram. We feel the need to make sure we are in moment-by-moment contact with the news. And we want to make sure the weather hasn't changed in the last five minutes. Along with this, we are all still in possession of wandering hearts. Things in our lives rise to levels of importance way beyond their true importance. Temptations seduce and seize us. Our desires wander off God's pathway. Envy sows seeds of doubt and bitterness in our hearts. Spiritual amnesia grips us; in the busyness of life we forget who we are and what we have been given. Our devotional lives are kidnapped by the tyranny of the urgent. What we want collides with what God wants for us. And the gap enlarges between what we say we believe and how we actually live.

Fasting can be spiritually arresting, a divine interruption that is one of God's tools to call us back to remember, to confess, to rest, to commit, and to celebrate. Fasting is one of the ways God reaches down into our frenetic lives and pulls us out to be closer to him. Fasting is much more of a welcome than it is a regulation. It is a gift from a God who knows us; he knows how we operate, what we face, and what we need. Fasting is God's invitation to all of his children to refocus, recharge, reengage, and repent.

So what is fasting? Fasting is giving up food (or something else) in order to focus on God and your walk with him (see Ps. 35:13; Ezra 8:23; Neh. 1:3–4; Matt. 4:1–11; Luke 2:37). We need to remember two important points. First, there is no magic in fasting. Giving up food won't instantly make you more godly. Fasting allows you to give yourself to other spiritual disciplines that will bear a harvest of good fruit in your life. Second, you don't fast in order to gain God's favor, but to help bring your life into even greater surrender to him and a greater appreciation of his favor. Fasting is spiritual warfare. It is one way that God has provided for you to fight for your own heart.

So how do you fast?

1. *Give yourself to prayer.* One of the primary purposes of fasting is to be able to give yourself more fully to prayer. The normal routines of food selection, preparation, and eating are replaced by new routines of prayer. It is this more focused communion with God that produces some of fasting's best fruit.

2. *Don't make a show of it.* Fast in private. Don't announce it. Don't broadcast it after. Pride in fasting robs fasting of its spiritual benefit. Seek God; don't seek the approval of others for seeking God in this way.

3. *Bathe yourself in God's word.* Fasting can give you time to meditate on God's word. In our busy lives, most of us spend very little time in actual Scriptural meditation. Biblical meditation is not like Eastern meditation. In Eastern meditation you empty your mind. In Christian meditation you fill your mind with God's word, chewing it over and over again until you are digesting spiritual morsels you have never digested before.

4. *Make sure you're ready.* There are no spiritual benefits to damaging your body or putting your health at risk. Make sure you are physically, financially, and situationally prepared for whatever fast, for whatever period, you are about to undertake.

5. *Be quiet before the Lord.* Since fasting is about ceasing participation in a particular thing, your fast shouldn't be filled with activity. Fasting is a time to wait on the Lord. And as you wait, remember that for the Christian, waiting is not about what you get at the end of the wait, but more importantly about what you become as you wait.

6. *Confess what has been revealed.* As you seek God in prayer, as you meditate on his word, and as you are quiet before him, the Lord will reveal your heart. Fasting is a way to fight the spiritual blindness that affects us all. So be ready to confess new areas of sin, weakness, and failure that God has revealed as you have fasted.

7. *Make new commitments.* If confession is turning from the old way, then commitment is turning your heart and life to God's

new and better way. At the end of your fast, think about where God is calling you to new commitments of faith and discipleship where you live and work every day.

8. *Be thankful.* Thank God for how fasting is an indication of his welcoming, patient, perseverant love, continually drawing you into even closer, more heart-satisfying communion with him.

So, fast this Lenten season. Receive God's welcome to fight for your heart and to learn to rest in the grace of your Savior more fully and more deeply. You will be glad you did.

Reflection Questions ————————————————————

1. Do you usually think of fasting as "more of a welcome than it is a regulation"? What has colored your perceptions of fasting?

2. Do you fast? Why do you or don't you engage in this spiritual practice?

3. What benefits does or would fasting offer for you? In what areas do you long for more focus or spiritual effectiveness?

Read Matthew 6:16–18, and ask the Lord if he is calling you to fast.

DAY 25

Lent is not about what you will give of yourself to God, but about what he, in grace, has so bountifully given to you.

He had been caught in adultery. It was humiliating for him and devastating to his marriage. He didn't confess until he was caught. Jerry and his wife came to me for help. They both seemed to want to save their marriage. He spoke words of brokenness to me and seemed to be repentant. Mary was willing to hang in there as long as Jerry was turning from the entanglements of sin and turning toward his Lord and her with new commitments of faith. But as I continued to meet with them, I began to be concerned. Truly repentant people are overwhelmed with the rebelliousness and destructiveness of what they have done, while at the same time, they are blown away by the magnitude and consistency of God's mercy and grace. They tend to experience the love of God in deeper and fresher ways as they tend to embrace in new ways the truth that they could never do anything to earn that love.

But when I would meet with Jerry, the thing Jerry talked about the most was Jerry. He talked about all the things he was giving up for the Lord, the length and depth of his new devotional life, the Christian books he had purchased, and the new ways he was serving his wife. He kept telling me how he was "all in" for the Lord. The more he told me, and the more he patted himself on the back, the less I believed it. It wasn't, "God, be merciful to me a sinner," but rather, "God, look at what I am doing for you." He had an attitude of the heart that the grief of real confession and the humility of true repentance would never produce. When I began to write this devotional, I thought of Jerry, and here's why.

The season of Lent is about offering yourself to God in new or deeper ways. It's about new submission and deeper devotion. Lent is about mourning the ways your heart has wandered. It is about confessing the hold the world still has on you or the places where you have succumbed to temptation's draw. It is about identifying places in the heart where you need to give yourself more fully to God. There is a necessary self-focus to Lent because you are examining your heart, your life, your relationships, and your daily decisions to see where God is calling you to give something up or to take something up in devotion to him. Lent is about willing self-sacrifice as you pursue the one who made the ultimate sacrifice for you. Lent isn't a formal season of temporary sacrificial devotion, but rather an opportunity to address things in your life that need to be addressed but that get lost in the busyness and distraction of everything else you're doing. But here's what is so important to understand about Lent: it is not about what you are doing or are committing yourself to do for God, but about what he has done and is now doing for you.

The story of Lent is the world's most important and most wonderful generosity story. Lent is about one who not only lavishly gives what is desperately needed, but who also offers himself as the ultimate gift. But the story of Lent is not just about generosity; it is the one story where the giver and the gift are the same person. The hope and security of Lent is not to be found in the size and consistency of what you give to God; it is about the stunning gifts of grace he has given and will continue to give you. It is God's generosity that is primary and transformative, not ours. We love because he first loved us. We give because he first gave to us. We lay down our lives because he first laid down his. We are willing to suffer for his sake because he first suffered for us. We obey because in his obedience we are given hope. We fight temptation because he fought it and defeated it on our behalf. We are willing to humble ourselves and serve because he left the splendor of eternity, humbled himself, and served up to and through the point of death. Everything we ever give of ourselves happens only because of the primacy of his gifts to us. He is the ultimate giver. No matter how great our sacrifices or how much we give, we will never give to him the magnitude of what he has given us. As we seek to give ourselves more fully during Lent, every gift we give is a celebration of the transformative storehouse of what he has given us. Lent is all about sacrifice: his, not ours.

Pride in the sacrifices you are making not only crushes the spirit of this wonderful season of spiritual reflection and growth, but it also quenches the work that the Holy Spirit would do in your heart as you open it up to him. Pride doesn't mix well with the grief over sin that propels confession. Pride doesn't sit well with the humility that fuels true repentance. A self-congratulatory attitude turns sacrifice into a reason to convince yourself that you're pretty righteous after all, and righteous people don't need the divine sacrifice that this season is all about. Pride flips the Lenten season on its head.

Now, here's the struggle. Whenever you focus on yourself, even in examination and confession, pride lurks right around the corner. It is so tempting to take credit for desires, choices, and actions that you would have never taken if you had not been rescued and changed by God's grace. If pride is self-congratulatory, then it is also self-reliant. But the whole message of the gospel of Jesus Christ is that you and I were not created to be self-reliant, and in our struggle with sin, we have no ability to defeat what we need to defeat on our own. This is why the sacrifice of Christ was essential. He came to do for us what we could not do for ourselves, even in our deepest moments of sacrifice and devotion.

So in this season of new and deeper sacrifice and devotion, resist the temptation of turning the tables. That is, don't make the lavish gifts of another become about what you give. You can't stand at the foot of the cross and consider the magnitude of what was done there and hold onto the pride of personal sacrifice. Pray for grace to make every sacrifice, every gift given, a celebration of both the ultimate gift and the most generous giver.

Reflection Questions ───────────────────────────

1. Jerry's story illustrates an important test for genuine repentance. Would you pass the test? Is your repentance more about what you have done or what God has done?

2. In what ways does Lent often lead to pride?

3. What are some practical ways to guard yourself against the tendency for the Lenten season—and spiritual disciplines any time of the year—to become a source of pride?

Read James 4:6–10, and let it lead you to genuine sorrow over your sin.

DAY 26

Lent teaches us that sorrow is the only
pathway to a life of true joy.

If someone called you on the phone and said, "I have very bad news for you," you wouldn't say, "Oh, thank you, I love bad news!" No, your heart would sink as you waited to hear what you didn't really want to hear. No one longs for bad news. We all dream of a life that is an endless stream of good news. But the storyline of Lent is counterintuitive: if you want to receive the best news ever, you have to accept the worst news ever. Lent teaches us that sadness is the only road to deep abiding joy. It confronts us with the reality that hopelessness is the only doorway to sturdy, unshakable hope.

Rick and Emma's marriage was a big, chaotic, and often conflictual mess. They were in debt, and their house was in disrepair. Their communication went back and forth between dysfunctional and nonexistent. Their relationship with their children was adversarial. Their spiritual life was a series of cold, formal religious habits. When they had sex, it was a physical act lacking in intimacy. When I first sat with them, I was aware that there seemed to be little warmth between them. The only reason they had asked to see me was the debt. It had grown and grown until it had become nearly impossible to handle.

As I got to know them, what blew me away was that their marriage and family had been this bad for a long time. They had learned to live with the mess. They had become masters at working their way around the dysfunction and keeping it all together. In fact, as I listened to them talk about their life together in matter-of-fact tones, I was impressed that they looked at the mess and didn't see a mess. What should have stood out as abnormal and dysfunctional, looked to them to be normal and functional. They weren't crying out for help; they just didn't like having all those big bills to pay. They weren't desperate for change. In the middle of the mess, with bad news all around them, this couple was satisfied. If I had a magic button that I could have pushed that would have made their debts vanish, they would have been satisfied for everything else to stay the same. This dear couple did not see the evidence of the bad news that was all around them, so they were not hungry for the message of good news that could have transformed it all.

I am convinced that, for most human beings, satisfaction is a much bigger problem than dissatisfaction. Let me explain. We sinners have a scary ability to be satisfied with what shouldn't satisfy us. Or let me say it another way. We are all too easily satisfied. We are able to be satisfied with conditions that are way less than God's original design for us or what grace now makes possible for us. We are often okay with living with things that are not the way they were meant to be. We are like the family that has lived three years with a broken toilet or with a car that has leaked oil for months. We live with the messed-up ankle or the overly sensitive stomach. Instead of fixing things, we find ways to use them even though they're broken.

We see bad attitudes in our young children, but we excuse them away, telling ourselves that our kids are tired, teething, or a little bit sick. Bad things happen in our marriages that get dismissed as a misunderstanding or the product of busyness. We cut moral corners or step over God's boundaries, telling ourselves that what God says is not okay, will be okay after all. Like the couple who came to see me, we all have the ability to look at the mess and not see a mess. We all have places in our lives where we're all too easily satisfied. And here is how this is spiritually dangerous: when you are satisfied, you don't reach out for help.

The cross of Jesus Christ yanks us out of our satisfaction. If things were okay, God would not have planned all that he planned and controlled all that he controlled, so that at a certain time in history his Son would do for us what we all desperately need but could not do for ourselves. The cross of Jesus Christ is the result of God's dissatisfaction with the condition of the world that he made and of the people that he placed in it. God was unwilling to be okay with what was not okay. So he moved, but not with the agenda to condemn but rather to redeem. God sent his Son to fix what was broken, to restore what had been destroyed, and to make dead things live again.

The cross is bad news for each one of us. It confronts us with the fact that there is something fundamentally broken inside us that we have neither the desire nor the power to fix without divine intervention. The cross calls us to admit that the greatest danger in our lives is to be found inside us, not outside us. Jesus came to be the perfect Lamb of sacrifice, paying the penalty for our sin. Why? Because the worst news of all is the bad news that sin not only distorts everything in our lives and separates us from God, but it also leads to eternal death. Sin is the bad news we have to accept. Sin is the thing that we have to confess. It is the bad news about all of us, and no one is an exception. You cannot understand the cross of Jesus Christ and be satisfied with pockets of sin in your life.

But the cross is also good news. The dissatisfaction of God is the hope of humanity. The cross tells us that God is willing to do whatever is necessary to fix what sin has broken. It tells us that God is going to move in love and pour out his rescuing, forgiving, transforming, and delivering grace. The cross welcomes us to look inside and around us and be dissatisfied. It welcomes us not to the dissatisfaction that leaves us hopeless, but a dissatisfaction that leads us to the foot of the cross where mercy and grace are found.

Lent reminds us that to be satisfied, to say you are okay and without need of help, you have to close your eyes and shut your ears to the bad news of sin that somehow confronts you every day. Lent welcomes you to bring a dissatisfied heart to your Redeemer, one who has seen and accepted the bad news, and to reach out for the help that he alone is able to give.

Only those who willingly receive the bad news will then seek and celebrate the good news. Are you too easily satisfied?

Reflection Questions

1. In what ways have you found this statement to be true: "For most human beings, satisfaction is a much bigger problem than dissatisfaction"?

2. What messes have you grown so accustomed to that you no longer notice them? What are you satisfied with that God isn't? What would change if you became dissatisfied with it?

3. How can God's dissatisfaction with sin and the resulting brokenness of this world lead us to hope and motivate us to action?

Read 2 Corinthians 5:16–21. How would these verses change your life if you let them inform your mess and brokenness?

DAY 27

What allows you to humbly and honestly look back
is the invitation to look up at the same time.

I wish I could say I asked you,
but I didn't.
I wish I could say I reached for you, but it didn't happen.
I wish I had thought that I needed help,
but my mind was elsewhere.
I wish I had sought your wisdom,
but I saw myself as wise.
I wish I had leaned on you,
but I thought I was standing up straight.
I wish I had cast myself on your grace,
but in the mirror I looked like someone who didn't need it.
I wish I'd begun each day with you,
but I was too busy.
I wish I had ended the night with you,
but I was too tired.
I wish I had spent more time in your word,

but I had people to see, places to go.
I wish I had looked ahead to a pathway I couldn't traverse
     alone,
but I was too focused on the here and now.
I am older now with more life behind me
than in front of me.
I mourn my
assessments of strength,
my appraisals of wisdom,
tagging myself righteous,
my quest for independence.
I regret the moments lost,
opportunities gone,
dreams now faded.
I would spend my last days
in the cloud of despondency,
beating myself up,
hoping to get back what is forever gone,
if it were not for your grace.
I would not be able to
look up as I
look back.
You went to the cross knowing
every choice I would make,
all that your mercy would need
to cover.
I can be honest about my choices.
I can confess it all,
and I can rest

because your grace is that
thorough
and your love has that much power.
Through the years I have learned
that to find the strength to
look back,
I need the grace to
look up.

Reflection Questions ────────────────────────

1. What are some of your biggest regrets in life? As you answer this question, do you consider spiritual regrets first, or as an afterthought?

2. Which of the regrets listed do you most resonate with?

3. Write your own "I wish" poem.

Read Acts 3:17–20, and let it refresh your heart as you repent and receive God's forgiveness.

DAY 28

In order to pray with confidence and hope,
you need to know who you're praying to.

Imagine that I have something embarrassing, humiliating, and potentially anger-producing to confess. Imagine I have been dreading having "the talk." Imagine that I have had nervous days and sleepless nights ruminating about what I would say and how I would say it, and wondering when would be the best time. And then imagine that I have two people that I have to confess to. The first person I do not know at all. I do not know what he thinks of me, so I can't anticipate how he will respond to my confession. The second person I know very well. I know that she is gracious, kind, patient, and forgiving. But most importantly, I know that she will love me and continue to love me no matter what.

Now think with me. Which person do you think is the source of my reticence and anxiety? The question is not hard to answer. It is obviously the person whom I do not know. Humble confession is always stimulated and ignited by the character and commitment of the person you need to confess to. It is his or her love for you that propels the honest transparency that fear crushes. It is not only pride that keeps us from admitting what we need to admit and confessing it without excuse or shifting blame—fear does too. So in this season of honest self-examination and humble confession, it is vital in those prayers to have a clear understanding of who is hearing your confession.

Listen to how the author of Hebrews talks about the one to whom you make your confession:

> Since then we have a great high priest who has passed through the heavens, Jesus, the Son of God, let us hold fast our confession. For we do not have a high priest who is unable to sympathize with our weaknesses, but one who in every respect has been tempted as we are, yet without sin. Let us then with confidence draw near to the throne of grace, that we may receive mercy and find grace to help in time of need. (Heb. 4:14–16)

It is hard to find more comforting words than these. You and I are welcomed to come to one who not only knows us, but who is personally acquainted with everything we face. Let me unpack the logic of this hope-giving welcome.

1. Your Savior sympathizes with you. Read the previous sentence again. The King of kings, the Creator of all things, the sovereign Lord of glory sympathizes with you. He doesn't look on you with irritation or impatience. He isn't mad at you. He never looks on you with disgust. He is tenderhearted toward you. But there is more. The passage above says that he sympathizes with your "weaknesses." It's an all-encompassing word, covering weaknesses of every kind. Let's be honest. You and I are a collection of weaknesses, held together and protected by grace. We all have weaknesses of mind, heart, soul, and body. None of us is independently strong. None of us is self-sufficient. The writer of Hebrews is telling us that our Savior sympathizes with our humanity. Why? The answer is clear: because in his incarnation he took on humanity. Jesus took on weakness so that weak people could run to him and know that they would be understood and tenderly cared for.

One of the most amazing and comforting aspects of Jesus's work is his humanity. He became what we are, so that we could find what we need in him. The humanity of Jesus is a significant part of what he offers us. He knows our weaknesses, he knows them deeply and personally, and he meets us in our weaknesses with a tender and understanding heart.

2. Your Savior went through what you are now going through. Not only did Jesus become human just like you, he also willingly subjected himself to this fallen and dysfunctional world. He knows where you live, and he understands what goes on there. He is not surprised by what you face, because he faced it. He is not shocked by the temptations that greet you every day, because he faced them too. There is no troublesome situation or relationship that you and I will ever face that he is unacquainted with. He came to the world we live in knowing what he would face. He was willing to be tempted in all the ways that you and I are, so that in our temptation we would have a place to run to where understanding and help would be found. Here is what this means. Every temptation that Jesus faced, he faced for you. Those temptations weren't in the way of God's redeeming plan. No, they were an essential aspect of it.

3. Your Savior went through what you went through without sinning. Notice how the writer of Hebrews is building a case, stone upon stone, that our confidence that help is to be found in Jesus is well placed. Jesus sympathizes with who we are because he became like us. He understands what we are dealing with because he dealt with it too. But those two things would be hollow comforts without the third foundation stone that the writer lays down.

You see, we need more than sympathy and understanding; we need help. It is wonderful to know that we come to one who is tenderhearted, but it's even more wonderful to know that he withstood what defeats us, he resisted where we give in, and he succeeded in places where we regularly fail. His track record is without blemish. He faced what we face without any wrong in thought, word, or action. He did what we could not do so that we would have help in our time of need. Every time he resisted temptation, he resisted for us. Every victory over sin was accomplished for us. He conquered sin, so that in his strength we would have the hope of conquering it too. His sympathy and his victory together are to cause us to run to him in our times of need.

4. When you come to him, he meets you with mercy and grace fit for that moment of need. Because of Jesus's understanding, sympathy, and victory, we can rest assured that when we come to him, we will get just the help we need, in just the way we need it, and at just the right time. This means that no matter what you are dealing with, no matter what you need to confess, no matter how hard it may seem, no matter how weak you may feel, and no matter how many times you may have failed, you are never without help or hope, because you have a high priest, and Jesus is his name.

Since sin is never defeated by denial and since confession is the doorway to getting help that really helps, fight fear and discouragement by reading Hebrews 4:14–16 over and over again. Commit it to memory. Keep reminding yourself that you don't need to be afraid, because your Savior is tenderhearted. And you don't need to be discouraged, because he has what it takes to defeat what has left you discouraged.

Reflection Questions

1. When was the last time you confessed to someone? How was that experience different from confessing to Christ?

2. How does God's sympathy toward your humanity affect your prayers?

3. How does knowing that Jesus faced all the same temptations you do and overcame them help you to better face temptation?

Read Hebrews 4:14–16 again, memorize it, and let it help you in your struggle against sin.

DAY 29

Jesus was born with a cross in his future, so that
there would be such a thing as forgiveness for sin.

I have had some really bad jobs. One Christmas vacation I worked as a garbage collector and between the cold, snow, and rodents, it wasn't my best celebration of the season. I worked one summer during college as an intern at a factory, cleaning the rust off exhaust systems with acid. I worked for a while as a "brickie," carrying concrete blocks to masons and mixing concrete when it was so cold outside that we had to add antifreeze to it to keep it from freezing before it could be used. I worked one job that was so dirty my mom made me undress on the back porch before I was allowed to enter our home. But the thing that made those jobs tolerable was knowing I wouldn't be doing them forever. They were hard, uncomfortable, unattractive, and physically exhausting, but I knew they were temporary.

I regularly think with sympathy about the people who have those kinds of jobs as their life work. I have deep appreciation for them; our lives are made better by their work. But when I think of them, I almost always think of someone else. I think of the one and only perfect person who ever lived whose job description was to die. Think about that for a moment. What if you knew that you would not just do dirty and uncomfortable work for a season or have a hard labor job for your whole life, but that the ultimate purpose for your existence was to die a cruel and unjust death?

What was in Jesus's future was not a surprise to him. The shocking nature of his capture, trial, and death was not a personal defeat. It was not a failure of God's plan. It was not a triumph of the enemy. No, the death of Jesus on the bloody cross was a personal victory and a public indication of the complete success of God's plan. From before his first breath, the plan was that Jesus would enter this broken world, suffer its brokenness, live a completely perfect life in every way, and then die on that cross.

There simply was no other way. Because of the moral rebellion of sin, righteousness had to be accomplished and an acceptable penalty had to be paid. Christ's death and resurrection had to happen so the righteousness of Jesus could be given over to the account of those who could never be righteous on their own, and so forgiveness could be granted because a suitable penalty had been paid for their sin. In this way sinners could be forgiven and accepted into relationship with God in a move of amazing grace that did not at the same time violate God's justice. Listen to how Isaiah talks about this plan:

> Who has believed what he has heard from us?
> And to whom has the arm of the LORD been revealed?

For he grew up before him like a young plant,
    and like a root out of dry ground;
he had no form or majesty that we should look at him,
    and no beauty that we should desire him.
He was despised and rejected by men,
    a man of sorrows and acquainted with grief;
and as one from whom men hide their faces
    he was despised, and we esteemed him not.
Surely he has borne our griefs
    and carried our sorrows;
yet we esteemed him stricken,
    smitten by God, and afflicted.
But he was pierced for our transgressions;
    he was crushed for our iniquities;
upon him was the chastisement that brought us peace,
    and with his wounds we are healed.
All we like sheep have gone astray;
    we have turned—every one—to his own way;
and the Lord has laid on him
    the iniquity of us all.
He was oppressed, and he was afflicted,
    yet he opened not his mouth;
like a lamb that is led to the slaughter,
    and like a sheep that before its shearers is silent,
    so he opened not his mouth.
By oppression and judgment he was taken away;
    and as for his generation, who considered
that he was cut off out of the land of the living,
    stricken for the transgression of my people?

And they made his grave with the wicked
    and with a rich man in his death,
although he had done no violence,
    and there was no deceit in his mouth.
Yet it was the will of the LORD to crush him;
    he has put him to grief;
when his soul makes an offering for guilt,
    he shall see his offspring; he shall prolong his days;
the will of the LORD shall prosper in his hand.
Out of the anguish of his soul he shall see and be satisfied;
by his knowledge shall the righteous one, my servant,
    make many to be accounted righteous,
    and he shall bear their iniquities.
Therefore I will divide him a portion with the many,
    and he shall divide the spoil with the strong,
because he poured out his soul to death
    and was numbered with the transgressors;
yet he bore the sin of many,
    and makes intercession for the transgressors. (Isaiah 53)

What was in Jesus's job description as Savior?

- to be despised and rejected
- to have a life of sorrow and grief
- to bear our griefs and carry our sorrows
- to be stricken, smitten, and afflicted by God
- to be pierced for our transgressions
- to be crushed for our iniquities
- to take our chastisement

- to be wounded for our spiritual healing
- to carry our iniquity
- to be oppressed without defending himself
- to endure oppression and judgment
- to be cut off
- to have a grave with the wicked
- to experience anguish of soul
- to pour out his soul to death
- to be numbered with transgressors

This is what your Savior was appointed to do. This was his redemptive job description. This was the only way for forgiveness to be granted, eternal life to be given, righteousness to be granted, acceptance with God to be guaranteed, and saving grace to be unleashed. He came willingly, and did it all without the faintest grumble or the smallest complaint. Jesus knew that his suffering would be temporary but the fruit would be eternal, and he was willing.

During this Lenten season, stop and consider the depth of the love of your Lord, that he endured this for you. He suffered the unthinkable so we could experience the unreachable. Now that's amazing grace!

Reflection Questions

1. What was your worst job?

2. How do you think knowing he had come to die affected Jesus's life and ministry?

3. How does the purposeful sacrifice of Christ transform your approach to your work and ministry life?

Reread Isaiah 53, and meditate on all that Christ did for you.

DAY 30

You can't repent of what you haven't confessed,
you can't confess what you haven't grieved, and
you can't grieve what you haven't seen.

I must admit,
I dislike the hardship of confession.
I avoid grief.
I don't like painful moments of regret.
I don't like thinking about my sin.
I want to follow you,
but free from the need to admit failure.
Your grace isn't a backroom,
under-the-table,
secret-handshake
deal you've made with me,
where you gloss over
my sin
and I walk away relieved.

You didn't make a deal;
you endured the cross.
You wouldn't call sin nothing,
when sin is a big
dark,
horrible,
rebellious,
destructive,
idolatrous,
self-aggrandizing,
law-hating,
death-producing something.
Any deal you would make would
empower the enemy,
encourage falsity,
violate your holiness,
negate your justice,
crush your grace.
Rather than a backroom deal,
you went public
on a hill outside the city,
where criminals die.
You put the ravages of sin,
my sin,
on display.
In a moment of
gross injustice
and public torture,
you hung between

heaven and earth,
suspended there by
justice and grace.
You not only took
the thorny crown,
the hard-driven nails,
the sword to the side.
You carried my sin
and the rejection of your Father,
as life seeped out of you.
You weren't accepting sin's victory;
you were declaring sin's defeat.
There is no denial permitted
at the foot of your cross.
The nails don't allow me to think
sin is nothing.
Your tomb opposes any notion
that sin is okay.
Your suffering and death calls me
to do what is unnatural for me:
to grieve,
to mourn,
to regret,
to confess,
to come out of hiding,
to admit my need for your grace,
to repent,
and to do all of these things
again and again,

with the knowledge
that a debt paid
is better than a bad deal.
Sin forgiven
is better than sin ignored.
Grace given
is better.

Reflection Questions ─────────────────────────────

1. How much of your prayer time is devoted to confession? Are you satisfied with that?

2. What could you do to make your times of confession more specific and meaningful?

3. How might meditating on Christ's sacrifice change your confession?

Walk through the passion account in Mark 14:1–15:39, picturing the scene as if for the first time, and let it lead you into a time of confession.

DAY 31

There is no defeat in the cross. Only
triumph is to be found there.

The life of Jesus was a death march. The life of Jesus was a victory parade. Both are true and must be held together. There
was no defeat in the righteous life and sacrificial death of Jesus.

The birth of Jesus was a victory.

The escape from the hand of Herod was a victory.

The humanity of Jesus was a victory.

The perfect life of Jesus was a victory.

The triumph over temptation was a victory.

The public baptism of Jesus was a victory.

The teaching of Jesus was a victory.

The healing ministry of Jesus was a victory.

The arrest in Gethsemane was a victory.

The trial and torture of Jesus was a victory.

The crucifixion with criminals was a victory.

The separation from his Father was a victory.

His death on a cross was a victory.

The resurrection was a victory.

His post-resurrection appearing to his followers was a victory.

His ascension was a victory.

Everything in the life, death, and resurrection of Jesus, even those things that appeared to be defeats, were victories. Each was a victory because each was done in fulfillment of God's plan. Each was a victory because it was done in fulfillment of prophecy. Christ did all these things as our substitute. He did them all on our behalf. He lived, for us, the life we could have never lived. He won, for us, battles that would have led to our defeat. He suffered, for us, so we would not suffer God's anger over sin. He conquered, for us, the final enemy, death. Yes, it was a life of suffering and death, but in it all was victory after victory. He came to conquer, and conquer he did. He came to reverse the course of human history, by victory after victory, until he could say, "It is finished."

The apostle Paul talks about the victorious life of Jesus in Colossians 2:

> Therefore, as you received Christ Jesus the Lord, so walk in him, rooted and built up in him and established in the faith, just as you were taught, abounding in thanksgiving.
>
> See to it that no one takes you captive by philosophy and empty deceit, according to human tradition, according to the elemental spirits of the world, and not according to Christ. For in him the whole fullness of deity dwells bodily,

and you have been filled in him, who is the head of all rule and authority. In him also you were circumcised with a circumcision made without hands, by putting off the body of the flesh, by the circumcision of Christ, having been buried with him in baptism, in which you were also raised with him through faith in the powerful working of God, who raised him from the dead. And you, who were dead in your trespasses and the uncircumcision of your flesh, God made alive together with him, having forgiven us all our trespasses, by canceling the record of debt that stood against us with its legal demands. This he set aside, nailing it to the cross. He disarmed the rulers and authorities and put them to open shame, by triumphing over them in him. (Col. 2:6–15)

Paul wants you to know that right here, right now, your life is rooted in the victories of Christ on your behalf. He wants you to know that when you are built up and grow, it is because of the victories of Christ on your behalf. He wants this identity to be the motivation behind everything you do. The Son of God left his lofty place and came to earth to suffer and die victoriously so that you would have not only a brand-new identity but also brand-new potential. If you are God's child, you are more than a husband, wife, son, daughter, father, mother, neighbor, friend, male, female, young person, older person, worker, retired, and so on. You are a child of a conquering King. You are a son or daughter of a victorious Savior. You have been raised and made alive. You have been forgiven, that is, your record of debt has been cancelled. Your penalty was nailed to the cross once and for all. This is who you are. This is how you are now welcomed to live, all because of the victory of Jesus on your behalf.

You don't have to live in timidity and fear. You don't have to give way to temptation. You don't have to surrender your desires to the things of this world. You don't have to chase after idols. You don't have to fear God's rejection when you have failed. You don't have to fear being honest about your sin, weakness, and failure. You don't have to look for identity where it can't be found. You can say no to the enemy. You don't have to fake righteousness you don't really have. You don't have to let anxiety rule your heart. You can rest in the unshakable love and forgiveness that is yours because of the victory of Jesus on your behalf.

I leave you with Paul's crescendo sentence: "He disarmed the rulers and authorities and put them to open shame, by triumphing over them in him" (Col. 2:15). On the cross, Jesus was robbing the enemy of its weapons. As Jesus was on the cross, the enemy was being put to shame. The cross was a triumph. Sin defeated. Forgiveness granted. Acceptance with God assured. Eternal life guaranteed. Victory now and in the world to come. This is your identity. Now go live it out.

Reflection Questions ───────────────────────

1. In what areas of your life are you experiencing defeat? Where do you feel stuck?

2. How can the truth that "[Jesus] won, for us, battles that would have led to our defeat" help you in your battle against sin and spiritual failure?

3. What fears do you need to claim Jesus's victory over? Do that now, in writing, and put them to rest.

Reread Colossians 2:6–15, and rejoice in Jesus's victory on your behalf.

DAY 32

*On the journey to the cross, not only is the heart
of Jesus exposed, but our hearts are too.*

I must admit that I like uncomfortable comedy, like *The Office.*
I like those cringe-worthy moments when you almost have to
turn away because you can't believe what the person is about to
say or do next. I think this is honest comedy. We all experience
those tense and awkward moments in our daily lives. We all find
ourselves in embarrassing situations where we would love to roll
back the cameras and be granted a retake. We have moments
when we are incredibly self-centered, miss the point completely,
or lack sympathy. We all find ourselves in situations where we are
more exposed than we want to be. We are all haunted by the video
replays in our minds. And we've all been hurt by others who said
or did the wrong thing at just the wrong moment.

Between the "already" and the "not yet" you'd better be ready
to have your heart exposed again and again, by words you wish
you hadn't said and actions you wish you hadn't taken. As he

journeys toward the cross, the heart of Jesus is exposed too, but it's not an awkward and embarrassing exposure; it's a thing of unparalleled beauty. Again and again, between his manger birth and his rough-hewn cross, you see the tenderness, the humility, the sympathy, the patience, the love, the faithfulness, the grace, and the generosity of the heart of Jesus. But as his heart is revealed, ours is too, and the contrast is not only deeply humbling, but it also exposes just how much we need the sacrificial death that this tender one is marching toward.

We clearly see the contrast between the human heart and the heart of the Messiah in this dramatic moment recorded for us in Mark 9:2–37:

> And after six days Jesus took with him Peter and James and John, and led them up a high mountain by themselves. And he was transfigured before them, and his clothes became radiant, intensely white, as no one on earth could bleach them. And there appeared to them Elijah with Moses, and they were talking with Jesus. And Peter said to Jesus, "Rabbi, it is good that we are here. Let us make three tents, one for you and one for Moses and one for Elijah." For he did not know what to say, for they were terrified. And a cloud overshadowed them, and a voice came out of the cloud, "This is my beloved Son; listen to him." And suddenly, looking around, they no longer saw anyone with them but Jesus only.
>
> And as they were coming down the mountain, he charged them to tell no one what they had seen, until the Son of Man had risen from the dead. So they kept the matter to themselves, questioning what this rising from the dead might

mean. And they asked him, "Why do the scribes say that first Elijah must come?" And he said to them, "Elijah does come first to restore all things. And how is it written of the Son of Man that he should suffer many things and be treated with contempt? But I tell you that Elijah has come, and they did to him whatever they pleased, as it is written of him."

And when they came to the disciples, they saw a great crowd around them, and scribes arguing with them. And immediately all the crowd, when they saw him, were greatly amazed and ran up to him and greeted him. And he asked them, "What are you arguing about with them?" And someone from the crowd answered him, "Teacher, I brought my son to you, for he has a spirit that makes him mute. And whenever it seizes him, it throws him down, and he foams and grinds his teeth and becomes rigid. So I asked your disciples to cast it out, and they were not able." And he answered them, "O faithless generation, how long am I to be with you? How long am I to bear with you? Bring him to me." And they brought the boy to him. And when the spirit saw him, immediately it convulsed the boy, and he fell on the ground and rolled about, foaming at the mouth. And Jesus asked his father, "How long has this been happening to him?" And he said, "From childhood. And it has often cast him into fire and into water, to destroy him. But if you can do anything, have compassion on us and help us." And Jesus said to him, "'If you can'! All things are possible for one who believes." Immediately the father of the child cried out and said, "I believe; help my unbelief!" And when Jesus saw that a crowd came running together, he rebuked the unclean spirit, saying to it, "You mute and deaf spirit, I command you, come out of him and never enter him again." And after crying out and convulsing him terribly, it came out, and the boy was like a corpse, so that most of them said, "He is dead." But Jesus took him by the hand and lifted him up, and he arose. And when he had entered the house, his disciples asked him privately, "Why could we not cast it out?" And he said to them, "This kind cannot be driven out by anything but prayer."

They went on from there and passed through Galilee. And he did not want anyone to know, for he was teaching his disciples, saying to them, "The Son of Man is going to be delivered into the hands of men, and they will kill him. And when he is killed, after three days he will rise." But they did not understand the saying, and were afraid to ask him.

And they came to Capernaum. And when he was in the house he asked them, "What were you discussing on the way?" But they kept silent, for on the way they had argued with one another about who was the greatest. And he sat down and called the twelve. And he said to them, "If anyone would be first, he must be last of all and servant of all." And he took a child and put him in the midst of them, and taking him in his arms, he said to them, "Whoever receives one such child in my name receives me, and whoever receives me, receives not me but him who sent me."

I have quoted this lengthy passage because it is the context that sets up the contrast between the heart of Jesus and the hearts of his disciples. Peter, James, and John have just experienced the shocking, heart-rattling glory of the transfiguration of Jesus, with Moses on one side and Elijah on the other. Here is the promised Messiah, displayed in glory, as the complete fulfillment of the Law and the Prophets. Here is the one who alone is able to satisfy the law's demands. Here is the one who alone is able to shoulder the hope of every prophet of old. Here is the hope of humanity. He is the hope that all that sin has destroyed would be made right again.

You have to wonder how Peter, James, and John carried this amazing scene in their hearts, a scene that they were commanded not to share with others.

After seeing Jesus in great glory, we next see him with great power as he does what is unthinkable: he raises a boy from the dead. There is no power in the universe greater than resurrection power. There is no feat that you could witness that is greater than taking the hand of a dead person, and by that act, bringing life back into that dead body.

But there is more. The disciples have been confronted with not only the glory of Jesus and the power of Jesus, but also the shocking reality that he was going to die and, after being killed, would rise again. It is all too much. This one of such glory and power would die? He would somehow rise out of death? You would think that the disciples' hearts would be filled with sadness at his death and that their minds would be filled with endless questions about what they'd seen and heard. You would expect that what they would be thinking about was Jesus. But here's where the contrast between the heart of Jesus and the hearts of the disciples is so great.

Jesus, full of power and glory, would not exercise this power to save himself, but he would offer himself as a sacrifice for the sins of others. He knew his glory and he knew his power but he also knew his calling, and he pursued it with joy. Glorious and powerful, he came not to be served but to serve, and to give his life as a ransom for many (Matt. 20:28). But what occupies the minds of the disciples? Awe in the face of his power? Grief at the thought of Jesus's death? Confusion as to his resurrection? No, they were thinking of something very different.

As they walked along the road, Jesus noticed a debate among them, so when they got to the destination, he asked them what they were arguing about. Embarrassed, not one of the disciples would answer the question, but Jesus knew. They were arguing about who was the greatest. They were not meditating on the messianic greatness they had just witnessed or ruminating over the news of Jesus's impending death; they were thinking about themselves.

As the greatest one who ever lived was willingly marching to a criminal's death, those journeying with him were questing to be great. I wish I could say that I can't relate, but I can. I sadly share this heart, and so do you. I like to be the center of attention. I like to have the strongest argument. I like to be in control. As long as sin still lives inside me, I will still have moments when I want to be great, and when I do, I demonstrate how much I need the grace of this glorious and powerful one, who did not save himself but willingly died to save people like me from myself. On the road to the cross, not only the heart of Jesus is exposed, but ours is too, and there's grace for everything that gets exposed.

Reflection Questions

1. What aspect of the disciples' reactions resonates with you? Where do you see yourself and your own sin in their behavior?

2. What characteristics of Jesus's heart revealed in Mark 9 do you think were surprising to the disciples?

3. What would have to change in your attitudes and actions for you to receive the kingdom of God like a child?

Read James 2:1–13. What insight does this passage add to the story in Mark?

DAY 33

The story of Jesus guarantees how your story will end.

How will this story end? This is the question in the mind of every human being.

How will my marriage end?

What will happen to my career?

Will my suffering ever end?

How will my kids turn out?

Will my investments pay off?

How will I get myself out of this mess?

Will I pass this course?

What will I have to deal with in old age?

What will I do after I graduate?

How will my ministry turn out?

Will the Bible turn out to be true?

These kinds of questions somehow, some way, haunt every human being. It doesn't take many years of life before you conclude that you're not only not in control of the big things in life, but also that there are very few things you actually control. It doesn't take long for the delusion of self-sovereignty to shatter. We're all also confronted with the fact that we live in a broken world that doesn't function the way the Creator intended. As a child, you aren't capable of theologically thinking this through, but you know messed-up and hurtful things happen a lot. As an adult, you adjust your expectations because you know the kinds of things that can happen in a fallen world.

In our smallness, we wonder if our lives will turn out the way we hoped and dreamed. My answer may surprise you. No, you won't get much of what you hoped for and probably few of your dreams. But here's the wonderful encouraging flip side of my answer. What you will get as God's child is way better than anything you could've hoped for and incomparably better than your brightest dream. Pay careful attention to what I am able to say. God doesn't guarantee you'll get your temporary dream; what he guarantees you is *forever*.

Because we are rational beings, we don't live life based only on the facts of our experience; we depend on our *interpretation* of our experience. We never leave our own lives alone. We are always thinking, interpreting, and rethinking. We carry assumptions with us and we draw conclusions, which color future observations. Let me say this another way: we are all storytellers, and our audience is us. We all compose a story of how we think our life should unfold; it's a story of what we desire and dream. And we all work to make the plot that we have written for ourselves come true. But grace introduces another author.

We are not actually the authors of our own stories; God is. He wrote our story ages before we took our first breath. Every situation, location, and relationship was written into the chapters of his book, by his sovereign hand. And by grace, he has embedded our story into the great and grand, origin-to-destiny redemptive story. We are now citizens of his kingdom; we now live in the shadow of his glory, and we are now called to live with his purpose in mind. Because our story has been embedded in his story, there is no doubt how our story will end.

Yes, we will suffer along the way. Yes, our hearts will go through seasons where they are laden with grief. No, we won't always be healthy. Yes, we will be weak and we will fail. Yes, loved ones will leave us. Sometimes we will go through seasons of want. We won't always be respected and appreciated. We won't always experience true justice. There will be chapters in the story that God has written for us that will be very hard. But we must remember two things. First, he has written himself into the story so that he will always be with us, giving us what we could never give to ourselves. Second, what your Lord has written for you is not less than the plot you have written for yourself, but infinitely more.

Most of us would be satisfied with temporal human happiness. We'd be satisfied with a good job, a nice house, a reliable car, a good church, a good marriage, successful children, and health and pleasure in our later years. But all of these dreams are not only self-oriented, but they are so dramatically brief when compared to the expansiveness of God's story. So rather than deliver our small and self-oriented dreams, God did something better: he sent his Son to earth.

Jesus was willing to come, suffer, and die so that we would have a way better story. He suffered so that our suffering would end forever. He lived a selfless life so that we would be freed from our bondage to ourselves, so that for all eternity we would know the liberating joy of living for something and someone bigger than ourselves. Because of his humiliation we will know the exaltation of living forever in the presence of the King.

Know today that no matter what you are going through, because of the grace of the life, death, and resurrection of Jesus, your little story has now been absorbed into his great story of victory over all that sin has broken. Because of what Jesus has done, you can rest in knowing the glorious way your story will end. In fact, because of the grace of Jesus, the end of your story is that it has no end!

Reflection Questions ————————————————————

1. Describe a time when God did something in your life that was not what you wanted or planned, but later you saw that his plan was better.

2. Functionally, who do you believe is the author of your story? You may mentally agree that it is God, but do you live that way? What evidence is there in your life that you submit to God's pen?

3. What parts of your story are you trying to write yourself? Are you willing to give God control? What are you afraid of?

Read Romans 8:31–39 as God's promise to you that even your heartaches are part of his plan.

DAY 34

Jesus's life saw no defeat, so we could know victory.

In your weakest,
most vulnerable,
seemingly helpless,
public-shame
moment,
hanging on a rough-hewed cross
between
heaven and hell,
nailed,
bleeding,
thirsty,
life ebbing out of you,
victim,
mocked and scorned,
you were a
conquering King—
not defeated,

the victor.
Seemingly defeated,
you conquered
sin,
Satan,
death.
Put to shame,
you were putting to shame
all who would shame you.
Not cowering
in fear,
you were parading your
sovereign glory,
unleashing your
transforming grace,
expediting your
redemptive plan.
The darkest moment ever
became the brightest moment ever.
The greatest defeat
became the greatest victory.
The moment of death
was a triumph of life.
You were where you came to be,
doing what you came to do.
You did not surrender
for a moment
so that we could
stand firm for a lifetime.

You did not give into
defeat
so that we would experience
victory.
Everything you suffered was
for us.
Every battle fought was fought
for us.
Every victory won was won
for us.
In your moment of
apparent defeat
you became forever
our victor.

Reflection Questions ────────────────────────────

1. Taking stock of the past thirty-three days, what is God convicting you of?

2. What changes have you decided to make, and how are those changes going?

3. What fresh perspective have you gained on what the death, burial, and resurrection of Jesus mean to you?

Read 2 Corinthians 5:14–21, and rejoice in the gospel message.

DAY 35

The march of Jesus to the cross was a
march of humility and triumph.

As we near the final days of the pre-resurrection life of Jesus, let's think once more about a familiar passage of Scripture. It is popularly known as the "triumphal entry." But the problem with familiar scenes is twofold.

1. Because a passage is so familiar, we often think that we know more about it than we actually do.

2. Because a scene is familiar, we don't give it the kind of attention we did when it was new to us, and this prevents us from learning more.

Let us consider Matthew 21:1–11, which records the final march of Jesus through Bethany and on to Jerusalem, and his death.

Now when they drew near to Jerusalem and came to Bethphage, to the Mount of Olives, then Jesus sent two disciples, saying to them, "Go into the village in front of you, and immediately you will find a donkey tied, and a colt with her. Untie them and bring them to me. If anyone says anything to you, you shall say, 'The Lord needs them,' and he will send them at once." This took place to fulfill what was spoken by the prophet, saying,

> "Say to the daughter of Zion,
> 'Behold, your king is coming to you,
>   humble, and mounted on a donkey,
>   on a colt, the foal of a beast of burden.'"

The disciples went and did as Jesus had directed them. They brought the donkey and the colt and put on them their cloaks, and he sat on them. Most of the crowd spread their cloaks on the road, and others cut branches from the trees and spread them on the road. And the crowds that went before him and that followed him were shouting, "Hosanna to the Son of David! Blessed is he who comes in the name of the Lord! Hosanna in the highest!" And when he entered Jerusalem, the whole city was stirred up, saying, "Who is this?" And the crowds said, "This is the prophet Jesus, from Nazareth of Galilee."

This is perhaps one of the most layered passages in Scripture. So much more is happening than what appears on the surface. There is more going on than Jesus entering the final stage of his work on earth in humility and majesty. There is more going on than a multitude worshiping him as the Messiah King. Let me suggest some words that unpack this moment.

1. Fulfillment. In this moment, Jesus is very aware of who he is and what he has been called to do. He knows that he is the direct fulfillment of holy and ancient prophecies. He is acting not with random spontaneity, but with a careful sense of who he is and the detailed specifics of what he has been called to do. He is not caught up in the moment, but rather motivated by an ancient and sovereign plan that he would be in this moment, at this place, doing these specific things. His heart is not moved by popular acclaim but by the will of his Father. What he does and what he directs the disciples to do is done with a spirit of calling, submission, and active obedience.

2. *Humility.* Jesus, riding on the colt of a donkey, is not playing to the crowd. He is the King of kings, the Lord of lords. He has come to sit on the throne of David to set up a kingdom that will have no end, yet this moment is not about him. It's not about how much the crowd loves him. It's not about how big the crowd is or how exuberant their celebration is. This moment is about one thing: the redemptive mission that was the reason for his birth, his righteous life, everything he taught, every miraculous act, his final trip to Jerusalem, his trial, his suffering, his death, and his resurrection. He did not come to collect followers who would deliver fame and power to him. He came to seek and to save the lost, and to do that, he had to be willing to humble himself, suffer, and die. The greatest man who ever lived was also the humblest man who ever lived.

3. *Majesty.* At the very same time, this moment in the life of Jesus is colored with glory and majesty. This is the King of kings. This is the promised Messiah. This is the Son of David. Here comes a conquering King. From that horrible moment of disobedience in the garden, humanity has cried for the coming of this King. He is coming to defeat what we could not defeat.

He is coming to give what we could never earn. He is coming to reign forever and ever and, in his reign, to fix everything that sin has broken. He has not come to defeat physical kings and to set up an earthly kingdom. He will not bring down Rome and sit on Caesar's throne. He will not deliver less than this, but infinitely more. He is coming to set up a global and eternal kingdom that will result in a new heavens and a new earth, where peace and righteousness will reign forever. In this moment, the King has come to take his rightful throne.

4. Misunderstanding. The crowd has no idea who Jesus actually is and what he has really come to do. They cry, "Hosanna" (which means, "Save us"), but the salvation they are looking for is temporal and political. They think the Messiah will set up an earthly kingdom that will break the back of Roman rule. This is why Jesus cannot be distracted by the adulatory desires of the crowd around him. He knows the hearts of people and how fickle they can be. Though on the road to Bethany he was heralded by cries of "Hosanna," in a few days in Jerusalem he will be cursed by a crowd of similar people, who will cry, "Crucify him." The crowd speaks in fulfillment of prophecy, but they speak about things they don't fully understand. Jesus came not to take momentary power, but to die in order to deliver eternal life. His crown would be made of thorns and his seat would be a cross. Soon the voices of the celebrants will be silenced and he will be reviled; this, too, will fulfill what the prophets had spoken.

5. Servanthood. As Jesus said of himself, "The Son of Man came not to be served but to serve, and to give his life as a ransom for many" (Matt. 20:28). He knew full well that the only pathway to his final kingship was death, and he was willing. He would not be diverted from the suffering that was his calling. He would do nothing less than give his life so that we would have life. Yes, he is the King, but he rode into Jerusalem to be the Lamb, that is, the final sacrifice for sin, and he did it with joy that was untainted by regret of any kind.

6. Eternity. The focus of the crowd is on the present, while the eyes and heart of the one on the colt are focused on eternity. He could have power now. He could call on angelic armies to preserve his life and to crush his enemies. He could exercise his power for his own escape, but he knows the result would be humanity's eternal doom. With the forces now pressing in on him, he comes with forever in view. He comes to gift the walking dead with life that would never end, and nothing will stop him from completing his mission.

This final ride of humility and triumph, on that borrowed colt, was a ride to the city of his death. Every aspect was done with the generations of souls who would put their trust in him in mind. He rode to his death so that we would reign in life with him forever. He did what he did so that, in a world made new again, we would sing hosanna songs to him forever and ever and ever.

Reflection Questions ——————————————————————

1. At the triumphal entry, humility and majesty met in perfect harmony. What impact does this joining of two seeming opposites have in the life of a believer? Why does it matter to us that King Jesus was both humble and majestic?

2. The crowds cried "save us" but didn't know what that really meant. In what ways do you try to ask Jesus to save on your terms?

3. The fickleness of the crowds is striking. In what ways do you cry "Hosanna" in one breath and "Crucify him!" in the next?

Reread Matthew 21:1–11, and try to put yourself in the scene—what do you see, smell, hear, and feel?

DAY 36

*Scripture records the anger of Jesus in the temple
to point to who he is and to clarify our values.*

And Jesus entered the temple and drove out all who sold and
bought in the temple, and he overturned the tables of the
money-changers and the seats of those who sold pigeons. He
said to them, "It is written, 'My house shall be called a house
of prayer,' but you make it a den of robbers." (Matt. 21:12–13)

How quickly the emotion of the drama of Jesus's last journey
changes! After the adoring crowds, the story takes a radical turn.
This is another one of those messianic vignettes that we think
we understand, but need to examine more closely. We see here
the holy anger of Jesus more than at almost any other moment
in his life. Do you know why he was so angry? Is it only about
commerce in the temple? Why does he call the sellers thieves?
What is the zeal that consumed him in this moment? Why did
he overturn those tables? What can we learn from our Savior's
holy anger? How can his zeal become our hope? These are the

questions begging to be answered as we consider this moment in Jesus's journey to the cross.

Jesus enters Jerusalem and takes no time to bask in the glory of the adoring crowds along the way. He knows he is on a mission of saving grace, and he knows how far that grace will extend. He knows that what is happening in the temple is not only a violation of his Father's house, of promises made to Abraham, but also of what he came to earth to accomplish. Without care for what people will think of him, he is driven by righteous values and holy anger to act on behalf of those unable to act for themselves.

Consider this meditation.

> The temple highlighted
> your holy zeal;
> what was there exposed
> your loving heart.
> More than an
> institution,
> more than a
> historic place,
> more than a
> religious edifice,
> more than a place of
> public worship—
> it was your
> Father's house.
> Anger filled your heart—
> holy,
> righteous,

grace-infused wrath.
The place for the
Gentiles
now a house of
commerce.
Sales tables replaced
praying places.
Animal sounds replaced
sounds of supplication.
This hallowed place,
now a den of robbers.
Market thieves had stolen
the Gentiles' only place.
Sellers violated your
covenant plan.
Merchants robbed your place of
its glory.
This place of divine love,
now a place of human greed.
No love for you.
No sympathy for the displaced.
No submission to your will.
No care for your saving plan.
Out of love for your
Father,
compassion for those
excluded,
commitment to promises made to
Abraham,

you overturned the plan of those who
stained the Father's house,
declaring the zeal of
your heart,
your holy mission,
your eternal position.
This zeal, then and now,
my hope.
Your anger, then and now,
my security.
Your promises then and now,
my rest.
Your grace, then and now,
my life.
For I know you will
remain zealous,
act in holy anger,
and overturn
the final table,
and I will dwell
safe
in your Father's house
forever.

Reflection Questions ─────────────────────

1. What was Jesus angry about? What were the moneychangers doing wrong?

2. What fills your heart with righteous anger? Where do you see modern-day moneychangers, and what are you called to do about it?

3. It's easy to put ourselves on Jesus's side here, but how might you be guilty of some of the same sins as the moneychangers?

Read Mark 11:15–19 and Luke 19:45–48.

DAY 37

*It should be a warning to us that the religious leaders of
Jesus's day could be so zealous and yet so completely wrong.*

It is striking to note that Jesus spent much of the time between
his entry into Jerusalem and his betrayal and death confronting
the religious leaders of his day. These leaders were trained, committed, active, and religious in every way, but they had distorted
the faith that had been passed down to them and were unable to
recognize that Jesus of Nazareth was, in fact, the promised Messiah of their hopes and longings.

Jesus knows he is on the way to his ultimate redemptive destination, Golgotha, and there is little for him to lose. So, with words
sharper and more critical than ever before, he picks away at the
very heart of the error of the scribes, Pharisees, and Sadducees. In
the stinging words of criticism, there is gracious warning for us.

In the scribes, Pharisees, and Sadducees we see false religion
masquerading as true religion. The humility of true religion has
been replaced by religious pride. The grace of true religion has

been replaced by legalism. The purity of heart found in true religion has been replaced by hypocrisy. The love of true religion languishes as the victim of all of the above. Jesus will not go to the cross without pointing out that what these religious leaders live and promote is the exact opposite of what he came to teach, to live, and to die for.

It is a loving and always appropriate warning to us that it is possible for you to be fully convinced that you are in the center of what is right and true and honoring to God, when actually you are in the way of it. Hypocrisy still lives, graceless legalism still lives, self-righteousness still lives; it is still easier to criticize than to patiently love, and to make demands than to serve. Where do these things still live? It is not enough to say that they still live in our churches. We must also humbly confess that artifacts of all of these things still remain in our hearts. The stinging critique of the religious leaders was not just for them; it has been recorded and preserved for us, so that we would not fall into the same errors.

Here is what is dangerous about false religion: it does a good job of masquerading as the real thing, with its zeal, its commitment to the regular habits of faith (prayer, giving, participation in formal worship, etc.), and its theological knowledge. But there is an even greater danger. False religion does not need a Savior. False religion is rooted in human righteousness. Rather than being broken, needy, poor in spirit, crying out for divine rescue, it comforts itself in evidences of its own righteousness. Think of the parable Jesus told of the prayers of the Pharisee and the tax collector in Luke 18. The Pharisee essentially told God he didn't need him, and he gave his good works as evidence of his independent righteousness, while the tax collector, overwhelmed with his sin, cried out for God's mercy.

True religion accepts the worst news ever, and because it does, it runs to the best news ever. True religion doesn't begin with a righteous resume. It begins with the devastating acknowledgment of sin. True religion mourns corruption within, which cannot be defeated without divine intervention. True religion never has human righteousness at the center. No, it has the amazing grace of a self-sacrificing Savior at the center. Its hope is never in what we have done for God, but in what he has so lovingly done and continues to do for us. True religion never produces self-assured religious pride. It never produces independent self-confidence. It never causes you to look down on those less righteous than you. It does not produce soul-crushing legalism. In the soil of true religion, humility, love, gratitude, grace, peace, and dependency on God grow.

One of the central ironies of human history is that the religious leaders of Jesus's day conspired to destroy the one who was their only hope in life and death. The one the Scriptures, which they knew so well, spoke of again and again was now in their presence, and they despised him and what he taught. While they wore their mask of righteousness, they sought to destroy the one who came to be our righteousness, wisdom, and redemption. On his journey to the cross, Jesus stops to expose a form of "godliness" that needs no cross.

Today, it is tempting for all of us to tell ourselves that we are okay when we're not okay. It is tempting for us to work to make ourselves feel good about what God says is not good at all. It is tempting for us to be unlovingly critical of those we perceive to be less righteous than we are. It is tempting to think we are spiritually mature because we are theologically knowledgeable. It is tempting to tolerate in ourselves actions and attitudes that we would condemn in others. It is tempting to see God as a means to an end, rather than the end all of our hearts really long for. It is tempting to reduce our Christianity down to formal, public religious habits, a faith that lives most vibrantly for two hours on Sunday morning. On the way to the cross, Jesus exposes us to his condemnation of the religion of the Pharisees because there are still seeds of Pharisaism in all our hearts.

In this season of reflection, sacrifice, and gratitude, I want to give you an assignment. Take time to sit down with your Bible and carefully read Matthew 23. As you read how Jesus confronts the Pharisees, read with an open, humble, and prayerful heart. Allow those words of confrontation to expose and correct you, and as they do, may you grow ever more dependent upon and thankful for your Savior, who was willing to die to rescue you from the one thing you could never escape on your own: you.

Reflection Questions ————————————————————

1. Contrast true religion and false religion. How can you spot them in your church? In yourself?

2. How have you seen or experienced this truth: "It is possible for you to be fully convinced that you are in the center of what

is right and true and honoring to God, when actually you are in the way of it"?

3. What practical things can you do to recognize and repent of false religion and embrace truth in your heart?

Read Matthew 23, and ask the Lord to convict you where conviction is needed.

DAY 38

Our hope is found in the fact that Jesus came to be the final Passover Lamb, not just a great teacher and a miracle healer.

And when the hour came, he reclined at table, and the apostles with him. And he said to them, "I have earnestly desired to eat this Passover with you before I suffer. For I tell you I will not eat it until it is fulfilled in the kingdom of God." And he took a cup, and when he had given thanks he said, "Take this, and divide it among yourselves. For I tell you that from now on I will not drink of the fruit of the vine until the kingdom of God comes." And he took bread, and when he had given thanks, he broke it and gave it to them, saying, "This is my body, which is given for you. Do this in remembrance of me." And likewise the cup after they had eaten, saying, "This cup that is poured out for you is the new covenant in my blood. But behold, the hand of him who betrays me is with me on the table. For the Son of

Man goes as it has been determined, but woe to that man by whom he is betrayed!" And they began to question one another, which of them it could be who was going to do this. (Luke 22:14–23)

If there had been no upper room, if there had been no fulfillment of the promises of the Passover, and if Jesus were not the final Passover Lamb, we would simply have no hope in this life or the one to come. It is impossible to overstate the importance of Jesus saying these profound words: "This is my body, which is given for you" and "This cup that is poured out for you is the new covenant in my blood." Here is Jesus, in that intimate final night with his disciples, saying, "I am the hope of fallen humanity, because I am the promised, spotless Lamb of God."

Just as the blood painted on the Israelites' doors in Egypt meant that the angel of death would pass over those houses, so all who put their trust in the Messiah Jesus are covered by his blood and therefore will not bear the punishment for their own sin. It's not enough that Jesus was a great teacher. If all he had done were teach truth, but had not shed his blood as the fulfillment of all the truth teaches us about sin and redemption, then we would be damned. If all Jesus had done were perform physical healings, then we would still be the spiritual walking dead. If all he had done were confront the false religion of the scribes, Pharisees, and Sadducees, but had not gone on to be the sacrificial Lamb that true religion requires, then we would be doomed. If all he had done were send his disciples out with a theological message, but had not been the historical, physical covering, by his shed blood, which that theological message requires, then we would be without hope and without God, sinners alone in this fallen world.

But he *is* the Passover Lamb. He *is* the fulfillment of the covenant promises of old. His blood covers and cleanses us. All human history marched to this moment in the upper room and the sacrifice of Jesus's life that would follow.

Whenever I read the account of the incredible moment in that rented room and hear Jesus talk of his blood that was about to be poured out, a hymn always comes to mind. Its words are near and dear to my heart. It was written in 1876 by Robert Lowry, who was a pastor in Philadelphia, the city where I live.

"Nothing but the Blood of Jesus"

> What can wash away my sin?
> Nothing but the blood of Jesus.
> What can make me whole again?
> Nothing but the blood of Jesus.

Refrain:
> Oh, precious is the flow
> that makes me white as snow;
> no other fount I know,
> nothing but the blood of Jesus.

> For my cleansing, this I see—
> nothing but the blood of Jesus!

For my pardon this my plea—
nothing but the blood of Jesus!

Nothing can for sin atone—
nothing but the blood of Jesus!
Naught of good that I have done—
nothing but the blood of Jesus!

This is all my hope and peace—
nothing but the blood of Jesus!
This is all my righteousness—
nothing but the blood of Jesus!

Now by this I'll overcome—
nothing but the blood of Jesus!
Now by this I'll reach my home—
nothing but the blood of Jesus!

Glory! Glory! This I sing—
nothing but the blood of Jesus!
All my praise for this I bring—
nothing but the blood of Jesus!

May you attach your sense of self, your meaning and purpose, your moral compass, and your hopes and dreams to the message delivered in that upper room and to the actual moment of sacrifice on that hill outside the city. And may every moment of sin, weakness, and failure be punctuated by you singing to yourself the ultimate answer to the ultimate question, What can wash away my sin?

Nothing but the blood of Jesus.

Reflection Questions ───────────────────────

1. What helps you enter into the true meaning of the Lord's Table, Jesus's blood and flesh *for you*?

2. In what ways are you trusting in something other than or in addition to Jesus's blood to save you?

3. How might it affect your day-to-day life if you really, deeply understood the importance of Jesus as your Passover Lamb, the way the Jews in Jesus's day did?

Read Matthew 26:17–30, and enter into the story.

DAY 39

We have hope because Jesus was willing.

I t is sad but unavoidably true: one of the marked characteristics of sin is unwillingness. Sin causes us to be:

unwilling to forgive
unwilling to obey
unwilling to serve
unwilling to trust
unwilling to give
unwilling to make peace
unwilling to be gentle
unwilling to persevere
unwilling to suffer
unwilling to submit
unwilling to sacrifice
unwilling to surrender

And the list could go on and on. We are often unwilling because of the selfishness of sin. Our "me-ism" puts us in the center. It makes life all about us: our wants, our dreams, our needs, and our feelings. Our struggle with the self-ism of sin will not be fully defeated until the sin inside us is no more. So, we face a world of difficulty. A marriage can't work if a husband and wife are unwilling to live in self-sacrificing, forgiving love. A parent-child relationship falls apart when the parent is unwilling to be patient and kind or the child is unwilling to honor and obey. Friendships don't work when the friends are unwilling to give and to serve. The workplace is hard and inefficient if the employer is unwilling to love his workers as he loves himself. Unwillingness to be temperate with food and drink will destroy your health. When we begin to examine our daily lives, it becomes clear that so many of the problems we live with are the fruit of our collective unwillingness to live as our wise and loving Creator has designed us to live.

God, in his vast wisdom, knew that the only way to rescue us from our unwillingness and its bitter fruit was to send his Son to be willing to be what we would never choose to be, to do what we would be unwilling to do, and to willingly die in our place.

This is why the following stop on Christ's journey to the cross is so striking, convicting, and hope-giving:

> And he came out and went, as was his custom, to the Mount of Olives, and the disciples followed him. And when he came to the place, he said to them, "Pray that you may not enter into temptation." And he withdrew from them about

a stone's throw, and knelt down and prayed, saying, "Father, if you are willing, remove this cup from me. Nevertheless, not my will, but yours, be done." And there appeared to him an angel from heaven, strengthening him. And being in agony he prayed more earnestly; and his sweat became like great drops of blood falling down to the ground. And when he rose from prayer, he came to the disciples and found them sleeping for sorrow, and he said to them, "Why are you sleeping? Rise and pray that you may not enter into temptation." (Luke 22:39–46)

This passage is a clear window into the willingness of Jesus. We find him in the garden of Gethsemane, facing what would crush any of us. Because he is God, he knows the redemptive plan. He knows he is facing injustice, torture, public ridicule, the cruelest death possible, and the rejection of his Father, all because he is going to load our sin onto his own shoulders and pay our penalty. In his humanity, he is quaking at the thought of it all, and he asks if there is any possibility that there is another way. Will you stop for a moment and imagine what would be going through your heart and mind if you knew you were facing such horror? You and I get upset at a flat tire, a sassy child, a mean boss, an unexpected bill, or a bad day. We go through a tough patch, and we begin to question the goodness of God.

But Jesus did not end his prayer with asking to be released from the sacrificial suffering awaiting him. Instead, he said to his Father, "Not my will, but yours, be done." That final sentence of Jesus's prayer in the garden gives every sinner who ever lived hope.

Jesus did not think of himself first. He was not propelled by his own comfort. He did not protect his rights. He did not demand to be accepted and respected. He willingly forsook all the things that we think are our just due. He forsook those things willingly and without coercion. He was willing because he knew what was at stake and he knew what the result of his self-sacrifice would be.

In that garden there was angst and fear, but there was not a shred of selfishness or rebellion. Jesus knew what he had been appointed to do. He knew what the culmination of his earthly work would be. In his humanity, it was a fearful thing to consider, but he had a submissive, loving, and willing heart. This moment of willingness is a moment of hope for all of us, who, in our sin, have lives that are marked by unwillingness. Our hope in this life and the one to come is never to be found in our willingness to believe in and follow him, but in his willingness to endure suffering and death for us. His willingness unleashes the grace we need to be forgiven and to become more and more willing to lay down our lives for his kingdom and his glory.

Reflection Questions

1. Think of your difficult or challenging relationships. Where has "unwillingness" of sin crept in? What could happen if you chose to be willing in those areas instead?

2. Imagine yourself in the garden watching Jesus pray—what are you thinking? feeling? wondering about?

3. What specific things was Jesus willing to do for you? List them out, meditate on them, and thank him!

Read Mathew 26:36–46, and praise Jesus for withstanding every temptation toward selfishness or comfort for you.

DAY 40

*The empty tomb stands as your guarantee of help
today and gives you hope for what is to come.*

Life in this fallen world is hard. It can be hope-defeating and discouraging. Sometimes it looks as if the good guys are losing and the bad guys are winning. Unexpected visitors enter your door, bringing the pain of various kinds of loss with them. Things you thought you could depend on fail you, and the promises of people you thought you could trust fail you. Our lives right here, right now, are a mix of joys and sorrows. It's frustrating how complicated things can be. Grief is an all-too-frequent visitor, and anger often bubbles up inside us.

The Bible gives us three reasons for the hardships of life that we all experience, whether in momentary frustrations or in prolonged seasons of pain and loss.

1. The world. The Bible has much to say about the world we all live in, but it warns us that the place that is our present address is dramatically broken and not functioning as the Creator intended. In Romans 8 Paul says our world is "groaning" as it waits for redemption (Rom. 8:22). You groan when you're in pain, you groan when you're frustrated, you groan when you're discouraged. Everything around us is not as it was meant to be. The world around you is like a car you need to get you from point A to point B, but has mechanical difficulties. It doesn't do well what it was created to do, so you have to face the daily frustration of wondering what will happen next. Each trip you take is marked with a bit of worry, and often your trips are interrupted by yet another mechanical failure. Such is the world we live in.

2. *The flesh.* When the Bible talks about the flesh, it's not talking about our physical bodies but rather our fallen nature, that is, our struggle with sin. Yes, we have been forgiven. Because of what Christ has done, God views us as righteous, and sin is no longer our master, but it is vital to remember that the presence of sin within us still remains and is being progressively eradicated by sanctifying grace. Sin is in us and all around us. Marriage would be dramatically easier if every husband and wife were sin-free. The same would be true of friendship, parenting, the workplace, government, your neighborhood, the church, the world of entertainment, education, and the list could go on. Sin complicates everything in our lives. Many of our daily frustrations and disappointments are the result of the presence of sin in us and in the people around us.

3. *The devil.* The apostle Paul ends his practical instructions in Ephesians 6 by reminding us that we live in the midst of a great spiritual war. Our struggle is not really with people, places, and things. No, what we wrestle with every day are principalities and

powers, "cosmic powers over this present darkness . . . spiritual forces of evil in the heavenly places" (6:12). There really is a great, dark, deceitful enemy, who prowls around like a hungry lion, seeking to devour us. Life is hard because life is war. All the things that we do every day and all our relationships are made more difficult because they take place in the middle of a spiritual war. There is a tempter, a deceiver, who will mess with your faith, seeking to instill doubt of God's goodness, faithfulness, and love in your heart. He doesn't have the power to remove your salvation, but he is intent on messing up your journey.

Because of the world, the flesh, and the devil, it is wonderful that the work of Christ on earth didn't end on the cross but with the shocking glory of the empty tomb. The empty tomb of Jesus is your guarantee of help here and now and of help to come. Paul tells us in 1 Corinthians 15 that the resurrection of Christ guarantees the present reign of Christ (see vv. 20–28.) What is the King doing right now? Paul says, "He must reign until he has put all his enemies under his feet" (1 Cor. 15:25). The sin that causes us so much heartache will be defeated. The enemy, who sows so much turmoil in our lives, will be defeated. Death, which seems to be the inescapable reality of our lives, will be defeated. The risen, conquering King will defeat these enemies, and the empty tomb is his promise.

But there is more. Paul tells us that the resurrection of Christ is a "firstfruit" resurrection (1 Cor. 15:20). This is such an encouraging word picture. When that first apple appears on the tree, the first grape on the vine, or the first bean on the plant, it is a guarantee of a harvest of many more to come. The empty tomb of Jesus guarantees another resurrection. We will rise up on the last day and be transported to a new world, a world where all things have been made new. There will be no more sin, there will be no more devil, there will be no more broken world, and there will be no more death. All pain, frustration, discouragement, and suffering will forever end. And as risen and fully redeemed beings, we will live forever in peace and harmony with our risen Savior King.

The empty tomb of Jesus is your guarantee that what you live with today will not always be. Every enemy that troubles your life right here, right now, will be under the victorious feet of your risen Savior, Jesus. His empty tomb guarantees the completion of the work. He will not quit; he refuses to relent until that last enemy is under his feet. Then, and only then, will he usher in his final kingdom and invite us into a world where all things have been made new.

The journey of Jesus to the cross didn't end with the cross but with the victory of the empty tomb, and that's a very good thing.

Reflection Questions ———————————————

1. How has what you've considered in this Lenten study informed your perspective on the suffering and grief inherent in life on earth?

2. How will considering Jesus's sacrifice make the triumph of Easter different for you this year?

3. What implications does the victory of the empty tomb have for your life?

Read the end of the story in John 20:1–29, and relive the joy of the first Easter.

SCRIPTURE INDEX